# CAREERS IN
# THE LAW
## Elizabeth Usher and
## Martin Edwards

## Fifth Edition

KOGAN PAGE
CAREERS
SERIES

# Acknowledgements

The authors would like to thank all those who helped, directly and indirectly, in compiling the five editions of this book – particularly those already in legal careers who were prepared to be the subjects of the case studies, and the professional bodies and employers who so willingly provided the detailed information on training and prospects.

First published in 1982 entitled *Careers in the Law in England and Wales*
Second edition, updated and revised to include Scotland and Ireland, entitled *Careers in the Law*, 1986
Third edition 1988
Fourth edition 1989
Fifth edition 1991

Kogan Page Limited
120 Pentonville Road
London N1 9JN

**British Library Cataloguing in Publication Data**

A CIP record for this book is available from the British Library.

ISBN 0-7494-0525-2

Printed and bound in Great Britain by
Biddles Ltd, Guildford and King's Lynn

# Contents

# Introduction

When thinking of careers in the law, most people think only of judges, barristers, advocates and solicitors and ignore the many other jobs that keep the legal system running smoothly.

In all courts there are clerks and administrators; every barristers' chambers needs to have clerks and typists; each solicitors' office employs legal executives, outdoor clerks and other clerical workers. In addition, there are those whose jobs provide services to the legal profession, such as court reporters and law costs draftsmen.

For some of these jobs you need to be highly qualified, for others you do not; but quite apart from any necessary training, there are certain common skills or attributes which are vital, whichever job you choose.

Law is man-made and created to regulate the behaviour and interactions of people. To enjoy a job in the law you are going to have to like dealing with people and helping them with their problems. Not all jobs in the law will bring you into direct contact with the general public (a barristers' or advocates' clerk, or a law costs draftsman, for example, will usually be assisting other professionals) but nevertheless, working with people plays an important part in any legal career.

You will also need to be able to communicate – a good standard of written and spoken English is needed in most of the jobs outlined in this book – and in any legal career you will have to be prepared to take on responsibility. In all these jobs a high level of integrity is required and you will also have to remember to be discreet, as you will have access to information about other people's lives and business dealings. So, whether you are a solicitor advising a client, or a secretary typing a letter of advice, utmost confidentiality must be observed at all times. Some careers are stressful, as time is short and the tasks responsible, but legal jobs at all levels are usually secure, and while the pay is often modest to begin with, it increases with experience, rising to above the going rate for similar but less specialised work.

Legal jobs tend to be desk jobs, so if you are keen on getting out of the office and travelling, a career in the law may not be for you. As the legal system differs between England and Wales, Scotland and Northern Ireland, and between these countries and the rest of the world, the qualifications you gain in one of the three jurisdictions of the United Kingdom may not readily equip you for finding work either in another part of the UK or abroad. Although it is always possible to retrain, in the case of solicitors, barristers, advocates and legal executives particularly, the opportunities to work other than in the jurisidiction in which you have qualified are limited. Before you choose a career in the law, you should consider not only the qualifications needed and the training involved, but also what the job will involve on a day-to-day basis and whether that is going to suit you.

You should also bear in mind that the legal system needs traditions to give a sense of continuity despite social change, and ceremony to reinforce its authority. As a result, there is a certain conservatism that attaches to legal work. Some may find the environment too hierarchical and staid; those who are happy in a legal career will probably find that the fact that they are in established and respected occupations is a positive incentive.

There is no doubt that the law, and the legal profession, are currently undergoing major changes. Many of the old barriers, such as those between the work of solicitors and of barristers, seem to be breaking down, and the openings for women and members of ethnic minorities are starting to increase. This book deals with the present state of affairs, but anyone thinking of a legal career needs to be aware that continuing changes in the nature of the opportunities available are highly likely.

It is a truism that any job will only give you back as much as you are prepared to put in – and so it is with legal work – but, whatever level you are at, you will find there is scope to learn more and take on further responsibility and as a result develop not only your career but, far more importantly, yourself.

# Part 1

# Chapter 1

# What is Law?

## Introduction

The law is a formal set of rules which regulate the way in which people behave, and the legal system of a country is the particular method by which that country's laws are created and administered.

Although England, Wales, Scotland and Northern Ireland are united politically, Scotland and Northern Ireland have entirely separate legal systems from the rest of the UK – both the laws, and the organisation of the courts and the legal professions differ, with the result that careers and training vary between the three jurisdictions. Thus, qualifying for a particular career in the law in one country does not always mean that you are qualified to practise in either of the other two. When choosing a career in the law, it is important to consider where in the UK you wish to work, and to train for that jurisdiction.

## Criminal and Civil Law

The laws in the UK give rights to and impose obligations on individual members of the community. These rights and duties fall broadly into two categories: those which are the concern of criminal law, and those which are the concern of civil law.

Criminal law upholds social standards by prosecuting activities which offend public morals, or generally held views of proper conduct. Crimes such as murder, assault and robbery, which both offend society's sensibilities and harm the individual, may be prosecuted by any member of society, although usually this task is delegated to the State.

Civil law enables individuals to enforce the obligations owed to them by other members of society. Some can be created by agreement between two parties (and the body of law concerned with this type of obligation is the law of contract). Other obligations are owed by each of us to every other individual: for example, we all owe an obligation to each other not to hold wild parties every night so as to cause a nuisance to others, nor to drive so negligently as to cause injury to other road users. Not all obligations are negative in nature; some are positive, such as the duty solicitors have to use proper care and skill in dealing with the problems of their clients. If any of these obligations are breached, the neighbour three streets away who has been denied sleep for a week, or the pedestrian knocked down by the careless driver, or the client whose solicitor has acted negligently, can all claim compensation from the person who has caused them injury, or possibly obtain an injunction or interdict to stop future recurrence of the injury. These civil wrongs are called torts in England and Wales and Northern Ireland, and delicts in Scotland.

## How Law is Made

Today the most important source of law in the UK is statute: in other words, Acts of Parliament. When a case comes to court and there is a statute which provides for the situation which has arisen, the rules laid down by the Act will be applied by the judge hearing the case. Statutes can create entirely new laws or can repeal old ones; they can change and develop the law in any area or they can draw together the existing statute and case law into a codified form for easier reference. Statutes cover both civil and criminal matters. Crimes from drug abuse to traffic offences, and civil matters from copyright to consumer protection have all been the subject of statutory intervention.

Where there is no relevant statute the judge will apply those rules of law that have been developed from custom and case law over the centuries. This source of law is called common law. In Scotland, which has a separate legal tradition, reference is also made to a body of legal writing (called the Institutional Writings) which dates back, for the most part, prior to the political union of Scotland with England and Wales in the eighteenth century.

## The Courts

The laws in the UK, whether created by judges or Parliament, are administered through civil and criminal courts. The courts are in a hierarchical structure which means that each court is usually bound to follow the decisions of the courts above in the chain, and that the decisions of the lower courts can be appealed to the courts above, and may be altered or reversed.

In England and Wales, civil cases are first referred either to magistrates' courts, the county courts, or the High Court, depending on their complexity and the amount of money involved in the claim. Criminal cases, on the other hand, are heard either by magistrates' courts or Crown Courts, depending on the seriousness of the offence involved and their consequent classification as 'indictable' or 'summary only' offences. Appeals from these 'courts of first instance' as they are known, are referred to the Court of Appeal (Civil or Criminal Division), the Divisional Court of Queen's Bench, or the House of Lords, which is the highest court in the land.

In Scotland, civil cases are first heard in the sheriff courts or the Outer House of the Court of Session. Appeals lie from sheriff courts to the Inner House of the Court of Session, either directly or via the Sheriff Principal. Appeals from the Outer House lie to the Inner House, and with leave it is possible to appeal from the Inner House of the Court of Session to the House of Lords in London, which by custom sits with at least two Scots Law Lords when hearing civil appeals from Scotland. Criminal cases are first referred either to district courts or the sheriff courts and appeals lie to the High Court of Justiciary, being the highest court of criminal appeal in Scotland.

In Northern Ireland the civil courts are organised on the English model. Cases are first referred through magistrates' courts or county courts and appeals from those lie first to visiting Judges of Assize or the Divisional Court in Northern Ireland. In certain cases appeals can be made to the Court of Appeal and the House of Lords in London, and certain matters arising out of the Northern Irish constitution can also be referred to the Privy Council in London. In Northern Ireland, criminal cases are usually heard by resident magistrates at petty sessions and from there it is possible to appeal to the county courts and, in more serious criminal matters, via the Assize Courts in Northern Ireland, to the Court of Criminal Appeal and the House of Lords in London.

## Barristers, Advocates and Solicitors

A notable feature of the legal system of the UK is that there are two distinct branches of the legal profession. Lawyers are either solicitors or barristers in England and Wales and Northern Ireland,

and solicitors or advocates in Scotland. These two branches are separate in their organisation, working system and training. Neither branch is able to undertake the functions of the other, though there may be a considerable overlap in the nature of their work in individual cases. The training of the two branches is separate. You have to choose to become either one or the other in one of the three jurisdictions and, although it is possible to move from one branch to another and from one jurisdiction to another, once you are qualified it is unusual to do so. If you are moving in either direction, or changing jurisdiction, you are usually required to undertake further exams or training.

The traditional view is that the relationship between a solicitor and a barrister/advocate is akin to that between a family doctor and a consultant in the medical profession. Certainly solicitors take instructions direct from clients, whereas barristers/advocates may not deal direct with the public and all their work has to be referred to them by solicitors. However, the traditional view implies that all members of the Bar (as barristers and advocates are sometimes collectively called) are each individually more specialised than the solicitors who refer work to them. This is not necessarily the case. In many firms of solicitors, while the organisation as a whole undertakes a very broad range of work, the individual solicitors deal only with certain types of case (some may specialise in conveyancing, others in litigation) and while it is true that many barristers/advocates are specialists, a great many, particularly in Scotland, have a very broad-based practice.

The principal differences between the two branches of the profession is that although solicitors can represent clients in the lower courts and before tribunals (for example, industrial tribunals), barristers/advocates have a right of audience before all the courts in the jurisdiction in which they have qualified. Whereas, for the most part, a solicitor's day is organised around his or her office, the barrister/advocate is normally involved in a far greater amount of court work. It should be noted, however, that solicitors are currently seeking wider 'rights of audience' in the courts.

Another significant difference between the two branches of the profession is that while solicitors can form partnerships in which the partners are self-employed persons, who can employ other solicitors and other staff, barristers/advocates cannot form partnerships. Barristers in England and Wales work from premises (known as 'chambers') with other barristers, but they remain in practice on their own. Barristers in Northern Ireland and advocates in Scotland do not rent premises in this way but work independently, from the Bar Library at the Royal Courts of Justice in Belfast and the Advocates' Library in Edinburgh respectively.

## Judges

Judges do not come from a separate profession. In other countries they often form part of the public service and are trained specifically for the job, but in the UK they are appointed by the Crown principally from among leading barristers/advocates, although some judges (particularly circuit judges) are selected from among the ranks of more senior solicitors.

Not all judges sit in formal court rooms, wearing wigs and robes. Recently there has been a growth in the number of tribunals which have, in effect, a judicial function, such as industrial tribunals and social security benefit tribunals. These often have lay members but the chairman of the tribunal is invariably a lawyer. Tribunals usually hear cases in less formal surroundings, and neither the tribunal members nor the barristers/advocates or solicitors appearing before them wear wigs or gowns.

It is perhaps worth mentioning that in England, Wales and Scotland, justices of the peace (commonly called 'magistrates'), who are the judges most people have dealings with, have no formal legal training at the time they are selected. Although in larger cities 'stipendiary' magistrates are selected from among experienced lawyers, most magistrates are laymen who receive training after their selection and hear cases with the aid of a legally qualified justices' clerk (see p 65). There are no lay magistrates in Northern Ireland and all magistrates there are either solicitors or barristers of at least seven years' standing. They are called resident magistrates or RMs.

## Women in the Legal Profession

Among judges, barristers, advocates and solicitors, men far outnumber women, particularly at the higher levels. It may be argued that this is not so much the result of direct discrimination as simply the effect of the long qualifying period, which leaves most women only a few working years between qualifying and the time when most wish to start a family. In the past, women have often had to choose between career and children. However, there is an increasing number of women now qualifying in both branches of the profession and in all three jurisdictions. Currently, about half the students passing the solicitors' final examination in England and Wales are women. Perhaps with the growth in the percentage of practising women lawyers, the profession itself will react more flexibly to their career patterns and encourage women who leave work to have families to pick up the threads later, and allow them to develop their careers to the full when they return to work.

*Chapter 2*
# Solicitors

## Introduction

The demand for solicitors' skills has grown steadily over the years. The number of solicitors practising in England and Wales is now in the region of 55,000. There are some 6,400 solicitors in Scotland and about 1,200 in Northern Ireland; in all three jurisdictions there has been a sharp increase in the number of admissions in recent years with also a marked increase in the number of women qualifying, so that now 50 per cent of solicitors qualifying in England and Wales, 40 per cent of solicitors qualifying in Scotland, and 50 per cent of solicitors qualifying in Northern Ireland, are women. Solicitors come from a range of social backgrounds and, although about 85 per cent of them are in private practice, others practise in commerce and industry, local and central government, and in the Magistrates' Courts Service (see Chapter 4). At present, certainly, an able solicitor, possessing both the academic and personal skills that the job demands, can fairly easily find interesting and satisfying work and expect to receive earnings comparable with those of other graduate professions.

The Law Society set up SOLCAS, the Solicitors' Careers Advisory Service, which is intended to increase awareness in schools, colleges, universities etc of the opportunities within the profession as well as of the various ways of qualifying. It has also published a code for good practice in solicitors' offices for work experience; some firms of solicitors in private practice are now willing to offer short-term placements for students aged 16 and over.

## Training

The training requirements for solicitors vary between the three jurisdictions of England and Wales, Scotland and Northern Ireland.

Solicitors qualifying in one jurisdiction do not automatically qualify to practise in either of the other two, but each jurisdiction provides for exemptions in their qualifying regulations for a solicitor already qualified elsewhere in the UK.

In all three jurisdictions, the profession is open to graduates and non-graduates alike, but it should be noted that well over 90 per cent of solicitors throughout the UK graduate before commencing their professional training. To qualify as a non-graduate is more time-consuming and more difficult, in that it necessitates studying while in employment, and many employers seem to prefer taking on trainees who have a degree.

**Training in England and Wales**
Training requirements are laid down by the Law Society (see p 123) from whom full details may be obtained, but if you decide to become a solicitor the first thing to think about is what route you wish to follow to qualify, as there are several to choose from. Although those entering the profession are mostly graduates, you do not need to have a law degree, or any degree at all. You may choose to start training immediately on leaving school with A levels, or you can start as a mature student (although this is very rare). The three main categories of trainees are: law graduates; non-law graduates; and Fellows of the Institute of Legal Executives.

*Academic Training*
*Law graduates*. A law degree obtained from a university or polytechnic will usually provide you with the basic academic qualifications for becoming a solicitor and will exempt you from taking the Common Professional Examination (CPE) (see below). However, not all law degrees cover the necessary 'core' subjects contained in the CPE and when choosing a degree you should check with the faculty and the Law Society to ensure that the degree you propose to take will provide the exemption.

*Non-law graduates*. If you obtain a degree in a subject other than law you will have to follow a course leading to the CPE which covers the core subjects taken as part of most law degrees, such as constitutional law, contract, tort, criminal law, land law and equity and trusts. Non-law graduates usually have to pass six papers and mature students eight papers. There are recognised courses leading to the CPE exams and details are readily available from the Law Society. Partial exemptions are available for holders of an acceptable qualification in magisterial law and for Fellows of the Institute of Legal Executives.

*Professional Training*

Having attained the basic academic qualifications appropriate to your category you can start the professional training, which for most people will consist of: (1) a final nine months' course; (2) the Final Examination; and (3) two years' practical training, ie service under articles.

Final courses, which are run by the College of Law and various polytechnics (see p 11), start in September of each year with a week of exams in the following summer. The course is divided into seven topics: conveyancing; consumer and employment law; wills, probate and administration; family and welfare law; litigation; the law of business organisation and insolvency; and accounts.

The Final Examination (FE), which consists of written papers, is a form of assessment requiring sustained concentration throughout the course and an ability to cram vast amounts of information. The effect is both physically and mentally exhausting! The course is practical in approach and is intended to equip trainee solicitors for the work they will do in practice, but while the exams include tests of the student's ability to analyse and draft legal documents, the examination system remains traditional. There is no continuous assessment throughout the course, and neither notes nor text books are allowed into the examination rooms. In addition, there is a limit on the number of times you can resit any exam you fail. You are expected to pass all exams at one sitting. If you fail not more than two, but pass the rest, you will be allowed to resit those two, provided you did not fail badly, but if you fail any paper three times you will have to resit each and every paper again.

It has to be said that these exams are not easy. Pass statistics of recent years suggest that there is a close relationship between the candidates' class of degree and their success in the FE. The secret of success almost certainly lies in regular and organised study throughout the course.

As from 1991, the FE will be replaced by a new Legal Practice Course. This will consist of practical training and will enable the student to learn about client interviewing, relevant law and the skills necessary to become a solicitor. It will be more skills-based and less knowledge-based than the present course.

**Training in Scotland**

Training requirements are laid down by the Law Society of Scotland (see p 123) from whom full details should be obtained.

In Scotland the profession is open to graduates and non-graduates alike and you can become a solicitor either by taking a law degree at one of the five Scottish universities which cover such courses, or by passing the Professional Examinations of the Law Society of Scotland. In either case, a student then has to undergo a further year of study in a university leading to the Diploma in Legal Practice, and complete a period of two years' practical training.

*Academic Training*

*Law graduates.* The five Scottish universities offering law degree courses are Aberdeen, Dundee, Edinburgh, Glasgow and Strathclyde. The Law Society of Scotland encourages students to qualify by way of obtaining a law degree since the degree provides a good general education as well as preparing students for their chosen career. To stand a chance of admission to a law degree course, you will be expected to have SCE Higher passes in English, mathematics and/or a science subject plus one or more foreign languages at good grades. Three-year courses lead to an ordinary degree and four-year courses lead to an honours degree. Those intending to qualify as solicitors usually obtain an honours degree, do the Diploma and then go on to their professional training.

*Non-law graduates and non-graduates.* The Law Society of Scotland's professional examinations are regarded as being equivalent in standard to a law degree. Only a small number of candidates in fact use this route of entry into the profession. There are no centres running courses leading to the exam; the Society provides encouragement by way of an extended syllabus and booklist for intending pre-Diploma trainees.

To be able to take the professional examinations, you must first obtain a pre-Diploma training contract for three years with a qualified solicitor practising in Scotland and, during that period, you must pass all seven of the Society's exams if you wish to make sure that you will be accepted for a university place to undertake the Diploma in Legal Practice.

Students are allowed a maximum of three years in which to pass the seven exams and if you have not completed them within that period, you will not be allowed to continue in training.

The Law Society of Scotland warns that it is often very difficult for students to find an employer who is prepared to employ them for the pre-Diploma training period, as most solicitors want to employ students who have already obtained the Diploma in Legal Practice.

## Professional Training

Whether you take a law degree or the professonal examination, you must then undertake one year's full-time study in one of the same five universities that offer the law degree courses. This year of study leads to the Diploma in Legal Practice. These exams correspond with the Final Examination which is undertaken by trainee solicitors in England and Wales.

## Training in Northern Ireland

Training requirements are laid down by the Law Society of Northern Ireland (see p 123), from whom full details should be obtained.

Entry into the profession now involves courses organised by the Institute of Professional Legal Studies. In the ordinary case, a student would undergo a two-year apprenticeship, during which he or she would attend at the Institute. An apprenticeship starts on 1 September and four months are spent in the master's office. The following year is spent at the Institute during the academic terms. The student would study full time during this period and would return to the master's office during academic holidays. The student would then be required to spend a further eight months in his or her master's office. Once all examinations have been passed and evidence given to the Law Society that the period of apprenticeship has been satisfactorily completed, a certificate of compliance can be obtained and admission will follow.

This is the usual method of qualifying which applies to law graduates. Graduates in other subjects would first have to obtain a certificate in academic legal studies, which can be obtained either part time or full time from the Faculty of Law, Queens University, Belfast. Other entrants, such as experienced clerks, can still be accepted provided they have a good general standard of education; they would undergo the Institute course on a part-time basis.

**Practical Training Throughout the UK**

Whether you are seeking to qualify in England and Wales, Scotland or Northern Ireland, you will have to undergo a period of practical training which is referred to as articles in England and Wales, traineeship in Scotland and apprenticeship or pupillage in Northern Ireland.

In all three jurisdictions the purpose of practical training is to enable the trainee solicitor to gain experience of the practical aspects of a solicitor's work. The student works under the supervision of a qualified solicitor, who is called the trainee's 'principal' in England and Wales and Scotland, and the trainee's 'master' in Northern Ireland.

The period of in-service training varies depending on whether you enter training as a graduate or otherwise, but the minimum periods are two years in England, Wales and Scotland and 12 months in Northern Ireland. You should check the details of requirements with the appropriate Law Society when commencing training.

During this period, you are an employee but you will also have a special relationship with the principal or master who has agreed to oversee your training. Except in Scotland, you are bound not to a firm but to an individual solicitor who is usually one of the partners. In England and Wales, only a solicitor who has held a practising certificate for the previous five years may enter into a contract with an articled clerk. In Scotland and Northern Ireland, a contract can only be made with a solicitor who has been in continuous practice for three years. However, you will probably end up working for and learning from most of or all the solicitors in the firm.

In England and Wales the deed of articles is signed by the student and the principal and is then registered with the Law Society. In Scotland, the student enters into a post-Diploma training contract with the principal which must be registered with the Council of the Law Society of Scotland. In Northern Ireland, an apprentice signs indentures with the master, which are lodged with the Law Society of Northern Ireland.

When it comes to finding articles, or an apprenticeship, the onus is very much on you. Some firms, and particularly local authorities, advertise vacancies in professional magazines, such as *The Law Society's Gazette* for England and Wales and the *Journal of the Law Society of Scotland*, as well as other journals (see p 119). The Law Society in London keeps a register of solicitors offering training (known as ROSET) and has an appointments registry with which you can register your name. However, there is no obligation on firms to use the registry and most fill their vacancies by waiting for prospective articled clerks to approach them direct. In Scotland, the Law Society also maintains a register of graduates seeking positions and you might also find it useful to look at the *Directory of General Services Provided by Solicitors in Scotland*. This is published every year by the Law Society of Scotland; it is a comprehensive guide to the types of work carried out by a wide range of firms throughout Scotland and will give you some insight into the type of work you would be likely to undertake if you manage to become a trainee with any particular firm. In addition, the Librarian of the Royal Faculty of Procurators in Glasgow maintains a list of students seeking articles.

Some firms visit universities and polytechnics to interview third-year students and it is worth asking if any such visits have been planned to the university you are attending. This practice is not followed in Northern Ireland. The Law Society of Scotland has suggested that firms do not accept applications until a student's third year of a degree, but certainly in England and Wales the advice given to students wishing to find articles is that it is advisable to try to sort out a place a year or so before you will be requiring it, particularly since large firms 'book up' a couple of years ahead.

In England and Wales, since 1979, the Law Society has required any solicitor taking on an articled clerk to provide experience in at least three out of eight given areas of law. These are: company and commercial law; family and welfare law; litigation (either criminal, civil or tribunal); local government; magisterial; property (including landlord and tenant); taxation; and wills, probate and trusts. Not all firms will provide the same options, and you should make up your mind as soon as possible during your training about the areas in which you want to specialise. Failure to gain experience in these areas during articles may make it more difficult for you to get a job in that type of work later on. Principals must be available to discuss general training problems with their articled clerks each month, and you will have to keep a diary of the work experience you are getting. You should be taught research, drafting and communication skills, and be given a grounding in general office and legal procedures.

As from 1993, trainees will have to undergo a four-week professional skills course as part of the training contract.

In Northern Ireland, the articled clerks are not formally required to cover specific areas during training.

The Law Society of Scotland provides guidance on the areas which it is appropriate to cover during post-Diploma training, but there are no longer any prescribed areas of training, and some trainees do in fact specialise to an extent during this period. Wherever possible, however, a general training is encouraged: there are prescribed areas of training for pre-Diploma trainees.

Articles/traineeship will give you the chance not only to put into practice the law you have learned in your various courses, but also to learn how to deal with clients, to come to grips with office administration and routine, and to understand etiquette. In the past, trainees paid their principals or masters for their training, but now money passes in the opposite direction. In England and Wales, the Law Society requires articled clerks to have an acceptable salary and can refuse to register articles if this is not forthcoming. The Law Society recommends a salary based on the grant of a university student grossed up for 52 weeks as a minimum guide to trainees' pay and trainees can now expect salaries comparable to those earned by most other graduates.

In England and Wales, once your training is completed and provided you are at least 21 years old, your name will be entered on the Roll of Solicitors and you will be eligible to apply for an annual Practising Certificate. You may also become a member of the Law Society, although membership is not compulsory. In Scotland a trainee petitions the Court of Session for admission and once the petition is granted, your name will be entered on the Roll of Solicitors kept by the Law Society of Scotland and again you will then be entitled to apply for a Practising Certificate. This is permissible after one year of training; however, only a restricted practising certificate is granted, allowing the second-year trainee to appear in the law courts. In Northern Ireland, you apply for a certificate of compliance, and again your name is entered on the Roll maintained by the Law Society of Northern Ireland.

*Case Study*
Rod

Rod is a 29-year-old articled clerk who turned to the law after originally working as a graduate in local government. He works for a 14-partner firm with five offices in the North West and a broad general practice.

My training over the two years of articles is divided between four departments: civil litigation, conveyancing, commercial and matrimonial law. (I have yet to start in the matrimonial law department.)

Initially, if one has not previously worked in an office environment, an articled clerk must familiarise him or herself with office procedures, and must also master the art of dealing with clients face to face.

My first six months were spent within the civil litigation department at one of the firm's branch offices. I soon became experienced in taking instructions from and advising clients, both legally aided and privately paying, in the fields of personal injury, consumer and contractual disputes. I attended many interlocutory hearings and often sat behind counsel during county court trials.

By the end of that time I felt reasonably confident with the work, but I then began a very different régime in the conveyancing department. This was equally busy, but perhaps more predictable, and I gained experience in dealing with house sales and purchases from start to finish.

Within the commercial department my training is based more on observing, sitting in on meetings, reading files and research, eg on points of company and employment law. There is understandably less client contact, as many business clients require their work to be handled at partner level. Even so, it is still possible to learn a great deal.

My only reservation about moving around departments is that, just as you become familiar with the work, it is time to move on. On the other hand, it is vital to obtain good quality experience over as wide a field as possible during articles, and that might prove more difficult in a smaller firm, for example one with little commercial work. At least my experience should enable me to make career choices on a reasonably firm foundation.

## Continuing Education

The Post Admission Training Regulations 1985 introduced a scheme whereby a solicitor admitted in England and Wales after 1 August 1985 was required to complete a programme of continuing education during the three years following admission.

Under this scheme, newly qualified solicitors have to attend courses approved by the Law Society and which have been accredited with points. The solicitor can choose which courses to attend but must acquire 48 points over three years, which in practice amounts to two days being spent on courses each year. In addition solicitors who qualified after 1 August 1985 also have to attend a compulsory half-day course on advanced accounts organised by the Law Society.

Newly qualified solicitors in Scotland are encouraged to attend post-qualifying legal education courses organised by the Scottish

Young Lawyers Association, the Scottish Legal Action Group and the Law Society itself, in the latter case generally at the expense of their employers. There is, however, no such formal compulsory programme of continuing legal education for solicitors in their early years of practice as has recently been instituted by the Law Society in England and Wales.

In Northern Ireland, newly qualified solicitors are restricted from practising on their own account, whether as sole practitioners or in partnership, for a period of three years after they are qualified. That period can be reduced to two years for someone who acquires sufficient points in the continuing legal education programme established by the Law Society of Northern Ireland.

## Working in Private Practice

It is worth considering in plenty of time what you would like to do when your articles end. It may take from three to six months to find the sort of job you want in the type of firm you want to work in, so do not leave it too late.

Some articled clerks and apprentices are offered work by the firm they train with, but since most firms will have several trainees qualifying at the same time you cannot count on this happening. Nor should you view the lack of such an offer as being very much of a reflection on your abilities. Staying on may not always be such a good idea as it first seems, as you may not be paid as much as you would if you moved, and you may find people still treat you as if you are unqualified. However, it can work out and has obvious advantages – you will know the office practice, and other members of staff will know what experience you have had and what help you might need.

Those who move firms on qualifying have to start on the round of replying to advertisements and attending interviews. In England and Wales *The Law Society's Gazette*, other legal periodicals, *The Times* on Tuesdays, the *Guardian* and *The Independent* on Fridays and several other newspapers carry advertisements for solicitors' jobs. In Scotland you should consult the *Journal of the Law Society of Scotland*, and also the *Scotsman* and the *Glasgow Herald*. In Northern Ireland your starting point may well be the *Belfast Telegraph*, the *Belfast Newsletter*, the *Irish Times*, or local newspapers (see p 119).

All three law societies have an appointments registry to which you can add your name and from which you can obtain the names of firms who have registered vacancies for qualified staff at all levels.

In England and Wales and Northern Ireland there are also commercial agencies who use a 'computer dating' system to match applicants to the jobs on their files. Their service is free to the employee but commission, which is related to the employee's salary, is charged to the firm once the employee has successfully served a probationary period (usually three months). Some firms rely heavily on agencies; others respond favourably to approaches made by applicants themselves.

Some jobs are found in the same way as articles, indentures or post-Diploma training contracts, namely by writing direct to firms who are not necessarily advertising for employees. This may be a successful exercise if you are approaching specialist firms or are looking for specialised work (such as employment law or tax), but you would have to be lucky and write to firms just as they were considering taking on new staff.

Having been an articled clerk or apprentice you will have come into contact with a number of people in the profession: other trainee solicitors, barristers/advocates and their clerks, court clerks etc. Don't forget your contacts when looking for a job. Tell people in the profession: they often hear of vacancies that might not otherwise be advertised. Later chapters deal with alternatives to private practice which you may find interesting.

## Salary

Your salary on qualifying can vary depending on your academic record and experience. It also depends on whether the firm is offering partnership prospects and considers you have partnership potential, what sort of work you will be doing, and where you will be working. If you specialise in commercial work, shipping law, computer contracts or tax you should expect to be offered more than solicitors specialising in conveyancing or matrimonial work. But this is not a hard and fast rule, and specialists of any sort in a city will probably earn more than general practitioners, wherever they practise. Also, it is generally, but not exclusively, the case that larger city firms will pay more than small firms in the country. The legal profession is, of course, subject to general economic pressures, and at times of economic stringency certain specialisations will fare less well and hence pay less well than others.

All that said, in England and Wales the Law Society suggests that a newly qualified solicitor could expect to earn £15,000–£17,000 pa in the provinces, more in London and around £17,000–£20,000 pa in large City practices. For solicitors of three years' post-qualification experience, rates of pay are in the region of £20,000–£22,000 pa in the provinces and £22,000–£30,000 pa in London, again with higher salaries being paid by the larger firms (1991 figures).

In Scotland the starting salaries are variable, each practice setting its own. In Northern Ireland starting salaries are variable but a minimum salary is imposed by the Law Society of Northern Ireland. Current levels are £2,080 (first year) and £4,500 (second year). These figures are subject to review.

Some employers will tell you what level of fees they expect you to earn for the firm; others have profit-sharing schemes by which their assistants are given a bonus related to the fees they earn over and above a fixed minimum, which helps to involve the assistant in the fortunes of the firm without necessarily creating a long-term commitment on either side.

Money is not all a firm will be offering. The package includes holiday entitlement (usually four weeks), and may also include medical insurance schemes, pension schemes, interest-free loan facilities and bonuses. You should bear in mind what the firm has to offer in terms of office environment, equipment and secretarial assistance. Remember, you are going to be in your office for 48 weeks of every year for at least eight hours a day. Therefore money cannot be your sole consideration when deciding to take on the job of a solicitor.

## Prospects

Assistant solicitors are employees and, as such, have no control over the organisation in which they work. Not all assistants want the responsibilities or ties of being a partner, and some remain assistants throughout their careers. This is a pattern which may occur with greater frequency, given the increase in the numbers qualifying. Traditionally, however, solicitors on qualifying have looked for jobs with partnership prospects.

## Partnership

Private practices are partnerships of solicitors. If you are offered a partnership it may be as an equity partner, that is a partner with a share in the capital of the firm who takes from the profits in proportion to his or her share. Particularly in larger city firms, it is more usual these days to be offered initially a salaried partnership, whereby you are still paid a fixed salary and do not usually take part in any significant decision making, but would be more involved than an assistant solicitor in the day-to-day administration of the firm.

Being a salaried partner is usually regarded as a stepping stone to a full partnership, allowing both parties a probationary period, since it is generally anticipated that when you become an equity partner you are making a commitment to the particular firm for the rest of your working life. That commitment is usually sealed by a capital contribution made by the new equity partner.

Occasionally, equity partnerships are offered which do not require the new partner to make any further contribution other than his or her continued efforts, but usually, if you want to be a full partner, you will have to be prepared to pay for the privilege. You may have to borrow money and it has been known for solicitors to earn less in the first few years as equity partners while they are repaying the loan than they did as salaried partners or assistants. Partners are, of course, self-employed.

The commitment to a partnership must be more than just a financial one. A partner in a small provincial firm recently stated:

> The most important things to ask yourself when you are offered a partnership are whether you trust those who would be your fellow partners and, secondly, whether you respect them for the work they do. You must like the geographical location of the firm, as you are going to be there a long time, and of course you've got to enjoy the type of work you'll be doing there. If those aspects of the deal are OK, you then go on to examine the financial proposals.

## Where to Work

The differences between city and country practices mean, to some extent, the differences between large and small firms. But this is not always the case: towns sometimes boast relatively large commercial firms, and all cities have their 'family firms'. However, some people prefer to work in a small community, of which they can become a part, where they can be closer to clients and come to know them and their families socially. Country solicitors often establish closer co-operation with other professionals, such as doctors, social workers, bank managers and the police, and this can be helpful in achieving quick and efficient results for the client. Generally, the pressures of a country practice are less, if only because the working environment is more pleasant and work is more integrated with the rest of life. Some people may find working in the country too claustrophobic for their tastes, and certainly, whatever you do, it is difficult to remain anonymous. If you want to keep your options open, it is probably best to work in a city at first and move out to the country later.

## The Type of Firm

When choosing a firm at any stage in your career you should think carefully about what sort of firm you want to join; large or small, specialised or general. In London a large firm would be one with 30 partners or more; one with only 15 partners would be regarded as medium sized. In the provinces a 15- partner firm would be thought of as big. In Northern Ireland, partnerships of more than five or six solicitors are comparatively rare. Scottish practices average three to four partners, but this could be misleading because some practices have 20 partners or more, and about one-half have only one or two.

Larger firms tend to be more departmentalised which means that solicitors working in them tend to be more specialised too. Specialisation may appeal to you, and certainly it follows on from the academic background that many solicitors now have. Some, however, prefer their work to be dictated by the clients for whom they work, so that they deal with whatever problem the clients bring in. Large firms tend to be more bureaucratic but they can afford to provide employees with modern office equipment, extensive libraries, and additional back-up services that may prove necessary for cases that are too large for one person to manage without help. However, you might also find a large organisation impersonal: it will take a long time to get to know everyone else in the firm, and unless you are a partner you will certainly not be involved in the way the organisation is run. Even more irritating may be the fact that you might not even know how it is run.

Medium-sized firms can have the best (or worst) of both worlds, allowing you to specialise while keeping a fairly broadly based case-load. In a medium-sized firm, each partner will tend to have his or her own clients who will dictate the type of work to be done. In a small firm there are none of the problems of getting to know all the other staff, and many solicitors enjoy feeling that their work contributes to the profitability of their firm. You may also find that, in fact, you are given great responsibility earlier in a small organisation, because there are not a number of other assistants employed who are just as competent as you are.

Sometimes whole firms are specialised, and while they may provide an all-round service to their clients, their reputation is built on their work in one field in which the major part of their work is undertaken. Specialist firms come in all sizes and tend to be based in cities.

On the whole, salaries are lower in firms of two to four partners, and highest in firms of more than 15 partners. The size of a firm may, therefore, not only affect the type of work you do but also the amount of money you can expect to earn. The place where you practise is also relevant; earnings tend, naturally, to be higher in central London than in the provinces.

## The Type of Job

Within private practice there is a great diversity of types of work you can do. Solicitors tend to be divided into those who undertake non-contentious cases, which do not involve any court work (conveyancing, both domestic and commercial; probate; trust work; company and commercial; tax) and those who deal exclusively with contentious or litigious matters, which result in court cases (matrimonial work; criminal and civil litigation). To some extent the sort of job you do will be dictated by your experience in articles, but you can change direction at that stage or later if you are sufficiently determined and can persuade an employer to give you the chance to branch out into a new field. To give an indication of the range of work and the types of job you could aim for as a solicitor, four case studies are set out below.

*Case Studies*
Nicola

Since qualifying, Nicola has been working for a medium-sized (21-partner) firm in the City of London which specialises in maritime law.

> The firm is departmentalised to some extent, as there is an admiralty department, a commercial department and a conveyancing department, but other than that, although each partner has his own clients, the rest of the firm's work consists of a variety of non-contentious commercial matters and litigious work, all involving shipping.

My clients are ship-owners – banks and other commercial institutions of foreign nationals, especially Greek and Arab. I arrange ship finance and deal with a variety of disputes, particularly those related to charter parties. Because of the form of agreements entered into in the shipping world, the litigation tends to be by way of arbitration rather than through the courts.

Officially, my working day is 9.30 to 5.30, but I rarely leave before 6 pm and I have been known to work until the early hours when a job had to be completed. Shipping finance tends to involve you in a succession of short-term jobs. You receive instructions on Monday and are expected to produce all the necessary documentation by Friday, and you just have to meet that deadline. Because many of my clients are in different time zones I have to take phone calls at home, outside office hours on occasions, and I also have to be ready to travel abroad at short notice, though I view these trips as a perk. It is really quite unusual for a solicitor to get the opportunity to travel but I get away about once in two months, mainly to European capitals and ports. Usually I go to collect evidence, complete financing deals or attend arbitrations, and I normally only stay for two or three days, but I was once in Paris on an arbitration hearing for two weeks. Fortunately, most of the work is conducted in English, though some solicitors in the firm speak foreign languages.

I have found as a practising solicitor that, while you need your legal training to understand the clients' problems and find solutions for them, the actual process by which you achieve the desired results relies on your ability as an administrator as well as a solicitor. Being able to organise papers and people efficiently goes a long way towards making a good solicitor, and copying documents, distributing information and arranging meetings are major activities in my working day.

The amounts of money at stake in the cases I deal with are enormous, and if I made a mistake it would probably be a very big one. That gave me sleepless nights at first but, as with most things in life, as you gain experience you gain assurance, and you worry less.

After five years in practice I can really say I enjoy my job. It can be very satisfying to help people who live miles apart to arrange their business dealings by advising them about their problems and then going on to assist them to achieve a practical solution.

## Margaret

Since qualifying Margaret has developed her career as an advocate. Many solicitors undertake their own advocacy, particularly when it involves undefended actions or simple applications before the local magistrates, and Margaret has built up a practice that looks like a barrister's. She works for an established eight-partner firm in the East End of London, which probably has more commercial work than most firms in that area. Not unusually, it operates from several offices within a small radius. Including Margaret, there are three qualified assistants plus four legal executives.

The work I do is predominantly litigious, about 25 per cent of it being crime, and I also do some matrimonial work. All the crime, and 50 per cent of the matrimonial work, is legally aided; the rest is paid for privately.

In these fields I do as much of my own advocacy as I can. I wasn't trained in this formally – I just learned as I went along. In the mornings I go into the office and spend half-an-hour dictating letters and answering the phone, and then I go to court. I usually go to the local magistrates, or county court as it isn't really economical for me to travel too far from the office, as that would mean I couldn't pop back there in the lunch-hour or when the cases were put back in the lists or adjourned. When I get back in the afternoon, I catch up with my post and make time to see clients and counsel. I still instruct barristers, partly because a solicitor can only appear in the lower courts and partly because the cases I become involved in sometimes clash. In addition to my own cases I also do court work for other people in the firm. Often I am given papers on half-a-dozen matters in an evening that have to be dealt with in court the next day, which means I have to study the papers at home.

Officially, my hours are nine to five, but I regularly work late. I have become quicker at my job as I have gained experience but I still have to be prepared to work long hours and miss lunch – that is one of the problems with court work.

There is a lot of contact with people in my job. Although the commercial clients realise they don't need to see me to give their instructions, clients with personal problems of any kind often just need to talk to someone. Some clients are inarticulate, others are illiterate, and you have to be alive to these problems and make sure you understand what they want and ensure they understand what you are doing for them.

There are unpleasant aspects to the job. Sometimes you have to tell clients that they will be sent to prison, and you have to prepare them for that. If I didn't switch off when I went home I couldn't do the job, and I know some lawyers who find it difficult to leave their work behind them at the end of the day.

## John

John has been qualified for seven years, and has worked in several London firms, doing mainly litigation. He was offered an equity partnership by one of his employers but turned it down. He is now a sole practitioner in an inner London suburb, in a very general practice.

I wanted to have a choice about what I did and the way I did it. As an assistant solicitor one doesn't have that freedom, and even in a partnership there are constraints, so six months ago I put up a plate outside my door.

To be a sole practitioner you need to have been qualified for three years and you also need to find some money. If I didn't work from home I would have had to have found offices, and the rent and rates payable on them. In any case I've had to furnish myself with all the equipment you take for granted when working in an office – dictaphones, safes, filing cabinets, telephones, photocopiers and typewriters. As I am on my own I have an answering machine, as I cannot be in two places at once and it's important for clients to be able to get in touch with me. I found that having my own letter-heads printed was surprisingly expensive and, of course, there are postal and phone bills. I have part-time secretarial help at present, but as the practice grows I will need to employ a full-timer. The only thing that seemed relatively cheap was the professional insurance, which was only £50 a year as I was setting up on my own for the first time and had never been in partnership previously.

Before you go it alone you have to investigate carefully where your work is going to come from and, while you must be prepared to do any sort of case for the sake of a healthy cash flow, you must establish early on an area of work you can rely on to turn over quickly. For most people that will be either private conveyancing or legally aided crime. If you have been working for a firm before you start your own practice you may be able to take some of your clients with you, but only if you arrange that with your employers.

I am sure I work harder now than I did as an assistant solicitor, out of necessity: I need all the clients I can get and, if all their cases demand attention on the same day, I just have to keep working until I've finished. Although I can work as flexibly as the pressure of work allows, I can't take holidays without employing a locum and, while most solicitors have to be self-motivated, I suspect that not everyone would really take to working entirely on his own as I do.

## Andrew

Andrew works in Plymouth, a city which provides the regional centre for all of Cornwall and half of Devon. Like Margaret's, his practice is specialised, but in his case the work is exclusively non-contentious and he is one of three equity partners. There are three assistant solicitors and one unqualified clerk.

About two-thirds of my case-load consists of conveyancing; the balance is will drafting and other non-contentious matters such as drafting contracts and partnership agreements. By and large my clients are individuals and families, but I also work for local businesses. In common with most solicitors, the major part of my day is spent dictating and answering the phone. About 85 per cent of my time is spent on client matters and the other 15 per cent goes on office administration, including personnel work, looking after the library, and overseeing general maintenance.

My father was a solicitor but I never intended to follow him and I took an arts degree. However, I didn't want to teach and I became attracted to being a solicitor because the job combines the practical application of law with human problems, and it is the combination of the academic and the practical that I enjoy. In private practice, at any level, you can be your own master to some extent – your clients ask you for advice and you give it objectively. Having done so, it really doesn't matter whether or not they follow it.

All jobs have their disadvantages. In small communities there can be pressure on solicitors to conform to rather conservative norms, though Plymouth is large enough for me to have a private life as well as a professional one. The public on the whole do not have a high regard for the legal profession, seeing it as inefficient and over-priced, and you have to accept a bad press and justify your existence at parties! Any practice depends on goodwill, and so a solicitor has to be available to his or her clients. Holidays are invariably short, and I have little time to develop other interests. On the continent, lawyers seem to have better educated clients and they take long breaks, but I can't see that happening here in the foreseeable future.

To succeed as a solicitor, merely being a good lawyer is not enough. You have to be able to stand back from your clients' problems and see them, and help the clients to see them, in perspective. Objectivity is very important, but you must actually like people and be able to get them to talk to you – they won't if they feel you don't want to listen.

In the past, people with problems turned to their priest or their doctor: nowadays they turn to their solicitor. Many agencies are able to give much the same advice, and there must be a reason for people to come to solicitors rather than any other advisory service. Traditionally, as well as expertise solicitors give a highly personal service, and when people have problems it is important that they can turn to someone who knows them and who will be sympathetic but who will, at the same time, give clear unemotional advice in confidence. The solicitor's profession is hybrid, based as much on business acumen as ethical commitment, but I consider that the legitimate role of the solicitor is coming round to being the traditional one. Since clients can increasingly obtain advice from other sources, they will only keep using solicitors if they get more from them than just information about the law.

*Chapter 3*
# The Bar

## Introduction

There are at present over 6,000 practising barristers in England and Wales of whom about 800 are women. The Faculty of Advocates in Scotland has 450 members of whom 200 are practising advocates, and there are over 300 practising barristers in Northern Ireland. Barristers/advocates are often referred to as counsel or collectively as the Bar. Their training and the organisation of the profession varies in the three different jurisdictions, but the type of work they undertake is very similar. Most counsel are permitted to appear before the courts only in the jurisdiction in which they have trained, so, for example, if you train as an advocate in Scotland you would not normally appear in courts in England, Wales and Northern Ireland, although this is likely to become easier as a result of recent changes in the law.

## What Barristers and Advocates Do

The principal function of barristers/advocates is to appear in court and represent clients and plead their cases, although they also advise generally on legal problems. They cannot take instructions direct from members of the public, and they have all their work referred to them by solicitors (where litigation is involved), or other approved professions.

They are generally regarded as the specialist members of the legal profession, although some solicitors, particularly those in the larger metropolitan centres, also become extremely specialised, and many members of the Bar maintain wide-ranging practices throughout their careers, being equally prepared to undertake criminal or commercial cases. Usually, solicitors help and advise the client from start to finish, and counsel are only called in to represent the client when the case comes to court. Again this is a generalisation, as solicitors can, and do, represent their clients in the lower courts. Equally, barristers/advocates may be asked to advise at relatively early stages in cases which may, in fact, never come to court, and some counsel, for example those involved predominantly in chancery work, make comparatively few court appearances.

However, the majority of barristers/advocates, as well as spending time drafting written opinions and pleadings and other documents necessary in the judicial process, also spend a considerable amount of time representing clients in court.

Therefore, at the Bar you will have a rather different kind of working day from that of the average solicitor. All your researches, conferences and paperwork will have to be before and after court and, as most courts sit between 10 am and 4.30 pm, the working week for a barrister/advocate may consist of many early starts and late nights. However, you may not have enough work, particularly at the beginning of your career, and it is also difficult to cope with days when you have nothing to do.

## The Skills Needed for the Job

In all three jurisdictions, the job demands more from its practitioners than mere legal knowledge. A degree of physical and mental stamina is needed to keep up with the lifestyle and to withstand the pressures involved. You need to be determined to succeed and must be ambitious, as there has always been an element of healthy competition at the Bar.

To enable you to be in court most days, with a limited amount of time for preparation, you will have to develop an ability to assimilate facts quickly and also learn to be flexible enough to change from one job to the next with ease. You will also need to be able to think quickly on your feet. The exciting side of the job – the court appearances – hinges on mundane and thorough preparation, and to prepare well you will have to teach yourself to be painstakingly accurate.

## Being Self-employed

A factor to note, if you are considering a career at the Bar, is that barristers/advocates in practice are self-employed. Being self-employed has both advantages and disadvantages. Barristers/advocates are answerable only to themselves for the way they occupy their time, and they are able to assess directly the fruits of their labours. Theoretically, provided the work is available, an individual who wants more money simply works harder, and it is true to say that barristers/advocates, like solicitors, can earn more than most people. The corollary is that there is never a guaranteed income, and this can be a primary concern in the early years. Sometimes you will worry because you are too busy, sometimes because you are not busy enough. And even when the money is earned it may not be paid for a considerable time, sometimes for years. Yet right from the start, barristers/advocates have to pay all the expenses of running their own business. These include the costs of travelling to and from court; buying the correct clothes, including a wig and gown; buying books and periodicals; paying hotel bills if they are required to represent clients in other parts of the country; contributing to the running costs of the office from which they work; and paying a clerk (see p 80).

Being self-employed, barristers/advocates usually need the services of accountants to help sort out their financial affairs and ensure that all the necessary returns, including VAT, are made. All expenses are tax deductible but this is of little consolation when bills have to be paid far in advance of receiving any fees. Of the first £100 earned at the Bar a newly qualified barrister/advocate might reasonably expect to retain £40 to £50 after covering the necessary overheads, although it is fair to say that as your earnings increase the overheads become less crippling.

## The Bar in England and Wales

The Bar is, primarily, a self-regulating profession. The barristers' professional body is the General Council of the Bar, which governs professional conduct and also looks after barristers' interests, for example in negotiating with the Government suitable rates of pay for publicly funded work. It is to some extent the 'voice' of the Bar and comprises elected barrister-members who are backed up by a full-time Secretariat.

### The Inns

All barristers who intend to practise at the Bar of England and Wales have to be members of one of the four Inns of Court, which are in London. These are Lincoln's Inn, Middle Temple, Inner Temple and Gray's Inn. The Inns, which were originally more akin to colleges of law, serve several functions. Just as the three law societies are the only organisations that can admit students to practise as solicitors in the UK, so the Inns are the only societies that can 'call' students to the Bar in England and Wales to practise as barristers. In addition to providing the necessary authorisation to practise, the Inns provide their members, both qualified and unqualified, with a basis for their professional and social life. Each Inn has a library where its members can work and a hall where they can lunch and meet, and there is a tradition of members dining together in hall on a regular basis to promote and maintain contact with each other. The Inns also have their own extensive buildings in central London which are let to barristers and other professional tenants as offices.

There are various levels of membership in the Inns, members being either students, barristers or Benchers. Benchers, or more properly, Masters of the Bench, are the senior members of the Inn, and are either practising or retired barristers or judges, who govern the Inns. They are co-opted by existing Benchers and each year one Bencher is chosen as Treasurer or administrative head of the Inn, though the day-to-day administrative work is carried out by the Sub- or Under-Treasurer and a permanent staff.

## Joining an Inn

You can join an Inn when you are ready to start on the vocational stage of your training, or while still completing the academic stage (see pp 43–4). In practice, this means you can join if:

1. You are a law graduate about to start a vocational course at the Inns of Court School of Law.
2. You are a non-law graduate or a mature student who has successfully completed the Common Professional Examination (CPE).
3. You are a non-law graduate or a mature student who has obtained a Certificate of Eligibility from the Council of Legal Education, prior to commencing a course leading to the CPE.
4. You are studying for a degree and have passed the English language GCSE examination.

All the Inns provide the same facilities. They furnish a collegiate life for their members, and for students in particular they provide help and support in what is, for many, a novel and perhaps confusing environment. The social events arranged by the Inns can help students to meet others in the profession; there are student associations and officers to help newcomers. The Inns also provide sponsorship schemes which allocate students to barristers already in practice, so they can have a professional contact who can be approached for advice. The way in which any sponsorship works depends on the individuals involved, and the assistance students get out of the relationship is usually in direct proportion to the effort they put into it. Sponsors often dine with students, and can put them in touch with pupil masters (see p 48) and vacancies for tenancies. Students will usually find sponsors prepared to talk to them about their work and will perhaps allow them to read the papers on which they are working. This may be the first taste you will have as a student of what life at the Bar is like.

As well as helping you to make social contacts, the Inns can also give financial assistance to students and pupils. Each Inn provides scholarships, prizes and awards, not all of which are means tested. A loan scheme funded by the Bar Council and the Inns, and administered by the Bar Council on the recommendations of the Inns, can also help support pupils and young tenants.

Choosing which Inn to join is very much a matter for the individual. Lincoln's Inn is traditionally associated with the Chancery Bar whereas Inner Temple has possibly a more radical reputation. Middle Temple is generally regarded as having a strong Oxbridge connection, and Gray's Inn has a reputation for providing a particularly good social life. Some people will choose a particular Inn because of family connections or because they have friends who are members, but if you have no particular connection with any Inn you should approach the respective Treasurer's office and ask to look around before making a choice. A fee is payable for joining any of the Inns.

*Dining*
The tradition of members of an Inn dining together in the hall of the Inn dates back to the time when the Inns were colleges of law responsible for the legal education of members. Law was then read and commented on at mealtimes, and a student became eligible for call to the Bar when he had been a member of the Inn for three years and had accordingly heard law read for a minimum period. Although the Inns have now handed over their educational function to the Council of Legal Education and the Inns of Court School of Law, the requirement for all students to keep dining terms remains. Basically a student must dine in hall on three separate occasions during each of the four terms before entering for the Bar examination, and for eight terms prior to being called to the Bar, but students are now permitted to complete all

dining requirements within the one year of vocational training. This practice is known as 'double dining'. Details of dining terms should be sought from the Inn you join.

No one reads law at dinner any more, and the purpose of dining is generally held to be to encourage social contact between students and barristers. However, the success of this is limited by the fact that, except for Inner Temple, which has mixed dining nights on six occasions per term, on most occasions the senior members of the Inns are segregated from the rest, and relatively few barristers dine in hall when there is no requirement for them to do so. Students are more likely to meet other students and practising members of the profession when 'keeping terms'. However, dining does introduce students to the more formal aspects of life at the Bar. Each Inn has its own ceremonies and customs, and students have to learn the etiquette of the profession they are joining. Dining formally in hall and wearing a black gown may help to bring that message home.

**Training in England and Wales**
Training requirements change quite frequently and so before applying to an Inn you should always check the full details of the training requirements with the Council of Legal Education. The details are also set out in the calendar published annually by the Council, price £2.75 (plus 37p postage).

The Bar is now virtually restricted to graduate entry and the minimum requirement is that a student should have a 2.2 class of honours degree, although the degree need not necessarily be in law.

You cannot start training to be a barrister straight from school and the only exception to the graduate entry requirement is in the case of mature students, although since graduates are expected to have a 2.2 honours degree, applications from non-graduate mature students are subject to very stringent consideration.

To qualify for call to the Bar you must:

1. be at least 21 years of age and
2. be a member of an Inn and have
3. kept the required number of dining terms in your Inn and have
4. completed the basic academic training and
5. if you wish to practise at the Bar of England and Wales, have successfully completed the training at the Inns of Court School of Law which is a full-time course with course assessments and examinations, and

6. fulfil one year's pupillage after you have been called.

*The Academic Training*
A law degree, provided it has included the core subjects (see below), will provide you with the basic academic qualifications necessary for starting the vocational stage of your training and will exempt you from the need to obtain the CPE. To take advantage of this exemption you will have to apply to the Council of Legal Education within seven years of 1 October in the year in which you were awarded your degree.

If you have a degree in a subject other than law, are a graduate of an overseas university, or if you are a mature student, you will have to follow a course leading to the CPE. The course covers the same six core subjects as the solicitors' CPE, which are also usually covered in law degree courses, namely: constitutional and administrative law; contract; tort; crime; land law; and equity and trusts. Full-time CPE courses are run by several institutions which also offer law degree courses. If you are not a law graduate you will need a Certificate of Eligibility from the Council before you can start on the CPE course. You should be very careful to apply in plenty of time both for the certificate, if you need one, and for a place on one of the courses. Always check the last dates of receipt of applications in each case, bearing in mind that these dates do not always coincide – you could apply for your certificate in time, only to find it is granted too late to gain you a place on the course you had in mind. Local authorities may give grants for CPE courses and you should approach the local authority in the area in which you live.

*The Vocational Training*
The vocational course leading to qualifications for practice at the Bar of England and Wales is run by the Council of Legal Education at the Inns of Court School of Law in Gray's Inn. The Council makes it clear that applications for this course are entirely separate from obtaining Certificates of Eligibility or joining an Inn, though you should have applied to join an Inn before applying for a place on the vocational course, and you must be a member before you can start the course. Applications for the courses must be made to the Council by 31 March in the year in which you wish to reserve a place, and are given to those students expressing a *bona fide* intention to practise. If you are studying for a law degree or the CPE, you may obtain a conditional place on the course before completing the academic stage of your training, so that if you are

successful you can go straight on with your studies. You should approach your local education authority direct before starting the course, as you may be entitled to a grant; otherwise the fees are £3,400.

The aims of the vocational course, introduced at the Inns of Court School of Law in October 1989 for all those who intend to practise at the Bar of England and Wales, are to provide a practical training in the specialist skills required by barristers, and to ensure competence in those skills. This will be achieved through practice in the tasks most commonly performed by junior members of the Bar during the early years of practice and, most particularly, in the second six months of pupillage. Approximately two-thirds of class contact time in the course is devoted to skills training while no more than 40 per cent of all class contact time is spent acquiring new knowledge. All aspects of the course emphasise the need for a professional approach to work, and encourage the students to develop a respect for the principles of professional conduct.

The student's successful completion of the course is assessed in practical work, and in multiple-choice tests carried out during the year.

Skills which have been identified as relevant to barristers are those also needed in legal research; information management and problem solving; opinion writing; conference skills; negotiating; drafting; and advocacy.

In the course, knowledge can be divided into four areas:

1. That of which the barrister should have a *detailed* knowledge and understanding (ie adjectival law – the rules of evidence and civil and criminal litigation, and the rules of professional conduct).
2. That of which every barrister should have a *general* understanding and be able to recognise the consequences of particular courses of action (ie all the remedies which could be appropriate in a particular case; sentencing practice and procedure; the potential and growing impact of European Community law; the basic structure and impact of the taxation system; an ability to read and understand basic accounts; and recognition of the legal ramifications of the different forms of business association).
3. That of which every barrister should have an *overview* because either it may influence the way in which a case is being conducted (the potential impact of: social security law, the European Convention on Human Rights, conflict

of laws, the law of succession and legal aid for example); or because it is such a common field of practice for the junior practitioner that some awareness of the legal area is necessary (ie landlord and tenant law, family law, and sale of goods and consumer credit law).

4. That which the barrister should know about *two specialist areas* of law and procedure before embarking on the second six months' of pupillage (ie, in the field of General Practice, two specialist areas of law and procedure chosen from family law, employment law, sale of goods and consumer credit, and landlord and tenant law; in the field of Chancery Practice, two specialist areas of law and procedure chosen from trusts, tax and wills, conveyancing and real property, and landlord and tenant; in the field of Commercial Practice, European Community law, company law and the law of international trade).

The three terms (Autumn, Spring and Summer) which make up the academic year will each be of ten weeks' duration. The course is arranged to enable students to acquire knowledge of adjectival law and other areas of law at an early stage so that it can be used in the practical work upon which the skills training is based.

The assessment process aims to ensure that students have learnt such principles and rules as are deemed necessary for successful practice and otherwise to test that students have reached a competent standard in the practice of the skills which will be used in the second six months' pupillage. Three forms of assessment are used: (i) multiple-choice tests in order to ensure the acquisition of detailed knowledge in evidence and civil and criminal litigation; (b) in-course assessments of performance in the practical work in order to assess the acquisition of skills and the ability to use knowledge of adjectival and substantive law and rules of professional conduct; (c) final assessment by means of written papers and videoed performance, which are assessed primarily on the basis of skill, but which will also require an adequate demonstration of legal knowledge.

The Council has entered into an arrangement with Blackstone Press Limited for the publication of materials specifically created to support the skills and knowledge aspects of the course. These materials are published as a set of manuals and all students are provided with them and are entitled to use them in the final assessment.

*Call*

If you successfully complete your academic and vocational training, are at least 21 years old, and have kept the required dining terms, you are eligible to be called to your Inn. Having lodged evidence that you have complied with all the requirements, you will be asked to attend a simple ceremony in your Inn, when you will formally be admitted to the Bar. There is a fee (£75 at the time of writing) payable to your Inn on being called but again you may be entitled to a local authority grant to help with these fees.

You will now be a fully qualified barrister, but if you want to go on to practise at the Bar you will have to do pupillage in chambers before you can start to develop your own practice.

## Chambers

Barristers, though self-employed, work from offices shared with other barristers, which are referred to as sets of chambers. If offered a vacancy in a set of chambers a qualified barrister becomes known as a tenant. Tenants share the running costs of the chambers (such as rent, rates, heating and lighting expenses, stationery, telephone charges, and secretaries' wages). One barrister, usually the most senior, will hold the post of 'Head of Chambers' and it is with him or her that contracts for services (eg for the telephones, stationery and rent) are made on behalf of the chambers as a whole.

Barristers in chambers can provide each other with support both directly and indirectly. They can sometimes help each other by taking on work from one of their number who becomes too busy (a practice known as devilling in England and Wales. In Scotland the same expression is used to mean pupillage – see below). They may lend books or the services of pupils (see p 49) and they can also support each other by discussing points of law or tactics, and more senior members of chambers can assist newcomers with problems of practice and etiquette.

Sets of chambers are found in London and 32 other towns in England and Wales. The number of barristers in a set varies considerably from less than 10 to more than 30. In London the average number is around 20, but elsewhere the chambers tend to be smaller.

It is to the Head of Chambers that a prospective pupil must apply for pupillage, although in most large sets of chambers there is a pupillage committee which selects pupils from applications received. The names and addresses of Heads of Chambers can be found in the Bar list (see p 119).

## Pupillage

Pupillage is the final stage of training for those who wish to practise at the Bar. It differs from articles served by solicitors in that the pupil is already fully qualified. Some barristers never undergo pupillage because, for instance, they wish to work in government departments or industry (see p 62), and there is therefore no requirement for them to do so. As a pupil, like all barristers in private practice, you will be self-employed and therefore not paid a wage. In addition, for the first six months of pupillage you will not be allowed to take on work in your own right, so that during this period at least, you have to be self-financed.

Pupillage is served with a pupil master who is a junior barrister (the term applied to all qualified barristers of whatever age who are not Queen's Counsel – see p 55) who has completed five years' continuous practice. It is the pupil master who will direct your day-to-day learning but, as he will be in chambers with other barristers, you will come into contact with, and perhaps undertake work for, them.

Most barristers start work with their pupil masters as soon as they can after being called, but if you feel you want a break from your studies, the last time you can conveniently do so is before starting pupillage. In your year as a pupil you will probably make the contacts necessary to find a permanent post and if you hear of a vacancy you will not want to pass it up. Once pupillage ends, you are going to be too busy building up a practice to take much time away from chambers. There are also some very positive reasons for taking time off immediately after being called: gaining other experience for a couple of years can be very valuable to you as an individual, and working at something else for a while can also make a lot of sense financially, for during the first few years at the Bar you cannot expect to have a regular income.

The difficulty of finding pupillage should not be underestimated – there are few chambers and many young barristers wishing to practise. So if you are not intending to take a break after your finals you would be wise to start looking for pupillage either at the end of your second year at university or, at the latest, when you start your vocational course. If you are going to take a break, it is wise to try to arrange pupillage before you are called. It is important to keep following up all leads and to find out all you can about the work done in any chambers you approach, because the work you do as a pupil will determine to a large extent what you will do when you work for yourself.

Pupillage lasts for one year and is split into two very distinct six-month periods. For most people this means serving six months with two different pupil masters in two different sets of chambers. In the first six months you will not be able to work for yourself and the time will be taken up with assisting your pupil master with drafting, research, and accompanying your pupil master in court. You will also attend all the conferences held with solicitors and clients in chambers, and in doing so you will learn how to behave in your dealings with other people. Your pupil master will ask you to prepare pleadings and other documents, as well as preparing questions for conferences. A set of chambers will rarely guarantee to keep you on after the first six months and you may have to go elsewhere for the second half of your probationary year. Not all pupils serve the whole year in private practice, and a few spend three months of the second six months of pupillage in the office of a solicitor or a lawyer in the EC or as a marshal to a High Court or circuit judge. In the second six months you will be able to accept briefs to undertake simple matters in your own right, and so earn fees. The work you will actually be offered will be a spin-off from the work of more senior members of chambers; for example, if there is a volume of personal injury work, a less experienced counsel will be needed to attend inquests or magistrates' courts to deal with careless and dangerous driving cases related to the personal injury claims.

Barristers are not only to be found in London, and if you intend to work in the provinces it will probably be to your advantage to serve pupillage in chambers out of London. The work will tend to have regional differences and a barrister working in the provinces could expect to conduct a Crown Court case earlier than someone undertaking criminal work in the City.

London tends to provide pupils with experience in bail applications and small cases in the magistrates' courts, which in the provinces are usually conducted by local solicitors. The work out of London is generally less specialised, and provincial chambers may sometimes have difficulty in keeping larger commercial matters which often are referred to London chambers. However, if you are a pupil in provincial chambers, you will certainly stand a better chance of becoming a tenant and it is arguably easier to get more demanding work at an earlier stage.

As you will not be able to earn fees in the first six months, you must consider how you can finance this stage of your career. The Inns and the Council of Legal Education make a variety of grants, awards and prizes each year. Normally, however, you will have to anticipate living on family loans and overdrafts to a considerable extent during the first few years at the Bar. Pupils can also take advantage of the Bar Council's loan scheme which provides low-interest loans to promising barristers in their first two years at the Bar, repayable in the fourth, fifth and sixth years of practice. All the Inns contribute to the loan fund, and details of the scheme, grants and scholarships should be obtained from the Inn you decide to join. Remember, you will not only have to find the cash for lodgings and food: you will need to buy smart clothes for court and a wig and gown; books; and pay the cost of travelling to and from court just like any other barrister. With all these expenses it is not surprising that some pupils obtain their pupil masters' permission to teach part time during their first six months.

Once you start to earn fees the need for an overdraft will continue, as the money you earn will not come in as fast as you earn it. The solicitor instructing you is responsible for your fees but, in practice, your fees are recovered from the client or the legal aid fund when the solicitor presents the total bill. Delays can arise – particularly in cases where you have played only a small part at the start of an action which continues for some time (perhaps years) after you have made your contribution. Sometimes the solicitor is slow in finalising matters, and not all offices have a very reliable system for picking up barristers' fees on billing; sometimes your clerk will miss the fact that a fee-sheet has not been sent out or remains unpaid; sometimes the client is a slow payer. Whatever the reason, the effect remains the same – there is likely to be a gap between your earning money and receiving it.

**Finding a Tenancy**
When pupillage ends you will have to find a permanent place as a tenant. There are very few tenancies compared to the number of barristers qualifying, and finding a place is far from easy. There may be a vacancy in the chambers where you served your last six months and, if so, you would be very well advised to stay on. Most chambers have tenancy committees which decide who will be asked to join the chambers as a tenant, and if you have been working in the chambers as a pupil the committee will consider the academic standard you have reached and your personal qualities.

There may be no vacancies in your chambers when your year as a pupil ends and if that is the case you will have to look elsewhere. While you are looking, you may be allowed to stay on in the chambers where you were a pupil, as a 'squatter'. Sometimes squatters have to pay towards the running costs of the chambers, but rarely have a room to themselves. They are useful to the clerk, as they have more experience than the most promising pupils and can therefore undertake complicated cases if the tenants are too busy. However, the clerk will usually consider you for a job after the tenants and the pupils. If you cannot stay on as a squatter, and you cannot find a tenancy, it is not unusual to arrange a third period of pupillage. You will be able to work, but as your place is not permanent you will find it very difficult to start to build up a practice. Finding tenancies is not easy, and you must follow up all leads. Many chambers now advertise vacancies in the Inns. Some squatters are taken on later as tenants when a vacancy arises: a third, or even fourth, six months as a pupil may put you in touch with a chambers which will offer you a permanent place. However, the hard truth is that you cannot remain a squatter or a pupil forever, and if you finally cannot find a tenancy you will have to get a job outside private practice.

A significant number of those who complete pupillage never become tenants, and it should be noted that women have difficulties in this respect. Clerks may be concerned with the prospect of building up women's practices, and may think they will leave to have families. However, those women who are determined to practise and to find a way of combining career and family do find tenancies, and the degree of control a barrister has over the course of his or her day has enabled a growing number of women to have both family and career, rather than a choice of one or the other. For both sexes, competition for a permanent place is keen, but once you are a tenant you can start to try to build up the sort of practice you want.

## The Bar in Scotland

All advocates in Scotland are members of the Faculty of Advocates. The principal officer of the Faculty is the Dean who is assisted by other officers such as the Vice Dean, Treasurer, Clerk and Keeper. All these officers are elected annually and the Dean and his officers constitute the governing body of the Faculty, controlling professional discipline and etiquette in much the same way as the Bar Council does in England and Wales.

### Training in Scotland

A candidate for admission to the Faculty is known as an 'intrant' and all enquiries concerning the procedure and requirements for admission to the Faculty should be addressed to the Clerk of Faculty (see p 123).

In the same way as the solicitor in England and Wales is an officer of the court, so too is the advocate in Scotland. The procedure for admission, therefore, is partly controlled by the court and partly by the Faculty.

Initially as an intrant, you must present a petition to the court through the Clerk of Faculty, though this is a purely formal procedure. The court then, also as a matter of form, remits to the Faculty for matriculation of the candidate as an intrant. In order to matriculate as an intrant you will have to pay the matriculation fee of £75 and satisfy the academic requirements (see below). To be admitted to the Faculty you then have to pass Faculty examinations and also undergo professional training.

*Academic Training*

In Scotland you don't have to be a graduate to become an advocate, but in practice most advocates graduate before commencing their professional training. Most law graduates will already have obtained passes in most of the required subjects, namely Roman Law of property and obligations, jurisprudence, constitutional law, Scottish legal system, Scottish criminal law, Scottish private law, Scottish mercantile law, conveyancing, evidence and procedure, private international law, European Community law and two other subjects which the intrant can choose out of 12 options. Edinburgh, Glasgow, Aberdeen, Dundee or Strathclyde Universities will provide the basic academic training, but non-graduates, or those with degrees in subjects other than Scots law who wish to enter the profession, must first pass the Faculty examinations. The standard required by the Faculty examinations is equivalent to that required for a degree course.

*Professional Training*

Having either been exempted from the Faculty examinations by obtaining a degree at one of the five Scottish universities, or having passed the Faculty examinations, an intrant then has to obtain the Diploma in Legal Practice from a Scottish university in just the same way as a person training to be a solicitor in Scotland. In addition the intrant has to serve a period of 21 consecutive calendar months' training (12 if the intrant has a first or second class honours degree in Scots law) as, or on the same basis as, a trainee solicitor in a solicitors' office. The intrant then has to serve a period of full-time pupillage to a junior member of the Faculty practising before the Court of Session, and during the period the intrant must also pass a Faculty examination in evidence procedure, pleading and practice.

### Pupillage

In Scotland, pupillage is commonly called devilling and, as with pupillage in England and Wales, the trainee works with a practising member of the Bar, often referred to as a 'devil master'. The work of the pupil during this period includes looking at his devil master's papers, drafting opinions and pleadings, attending consultations, discussing cases with the devil master, attending court with the devil master and learning from him or her the rules of etiquette required of an advocate.

### Admission to the Faculty

Having satisfied all the examination and training requirements you may apply to be admitted to the office of advocate. Admission to the Faculty (akin to being called to the Bar in England and Wales), is a public ceremony in the Advocates' Library at which the Faculty approves admission of the particular intrant to membership. Immediately thereafter the new member appears before the Court of Session to be admitted to the Public Office of Advocate by signing the Roll of Advocates and, in addition, is invited to make the declaration of allegiance to the sovereign in open court. When you are admitted to the Faculty the traditional form is to refer to yourself as having 'passed' Advocate.

### Chambers

In Scotland, advocates do not join together in sets of chambers as they do in England and Wales. An advocate can have as his or her chambers the Advocates' Library in Edinburgh, which is normally where advocates are to be found when they are not out of town, or they may have their chambers at home if they are within one mile of Edinburgh's Parliament House.

Advocates' clerks (see p 84) and the advocates' secretarial services are both found at Parliament House. Both are employed by Faculty Services Limited and each of nine clerks serves a group of advocates known as a 'stable'. Faculty Services Limited was set up by the Faculty of Advocates as a private limited company to administer the rendering and collection of advocates' fees, to employ clerks and to provide a number of other services.

## The Bar in Northern Ireland

In Northern Ireland there are at present over 300 barristers in practice, of whom about one-fifth are women. The governing body of the profession in Northern Ireland, equivalent to the Bar Council in England and Wales, and the Faculty of Advocates in Scotland, is the Executive Council of the Inn of the Court of Northern Ireland. The autonomous body which represents the profession to outsiders (in the same way that the Bar Council does in England and Wales) is the General Council of the Bar of Northern Ireland.

Call to the Bar in Northern Ireland is the responsibility of the Honourable Society of the Inn of Court of Northern Ireland, which is organised similarly to the Inns of Court in London, and to which all barristers and intending barristers in Northern Ireland must belong. The responsibility for providing education for intending barristers has now been delegated by the Benchers to the Institute of Professional Legal Studies which is part of Queen's University, Belfast, which also undertakes the professional training of Northern Irish solicitors.

### Training in Northern Ireland

Training in Northern Ireland, in common with training for barristers in England and Wales and advocates in Scotland, is also divided into two sections, namely the academic qualifications and the vocational training.

### Academic Training

Admission to the profession is open to graduates only and in practice most Bar students have a law degree which provides the necessary academic qualification. If you have a degree in a subject other than law then you will first have to undertake an academic course at the Institute of Professional Legal Studies before you will be able to start on the one-year vocational course.

### Professional Training

In Northern Ireland there are no formal dining requirements such as are observed by the Inns in London, and once the prospective barrister has achieved the necessary academic qualification, the next stage is to undergo a course leading to the Certificate of Professional Legal Studies at the Institute of Professional Legal Studies at Queen's University in Belfast.

*Call*

At the end of the vocational course Bar students in Northern Ireland are eligible for call to the Bar, which ceremony usually takes place in September. Students are called to the Bar in open court by the Lord Chief Justice of Northern Ireland, but unlike advocates in Scotland they do not take the oath of allegiance nor do they become officers of the court.

*Pupillage*

As with barristers in England and Wales, a barrister in Northern Ireland, having been called, cannot practise or earn fees until he or she has served at least six months as a pupil of a practising barrister of not less than five years' standing.

*Chambers*

Barristers in Northern Ireland are self-employed but they do not join together in chambers or employ clerks as barristers do in England and Wales; rather they practise from the Bar Library at the Royal Courts of Justice in Belfast. In that respect the Northern Irish system is more akin to that of Scotland.

## Working in Private Practice

In whichever jurisdiction you qualify, when you start working in practice you will be referred to as a 'junior'. Some barristers/advocates remain juniors throughout their careers and the expression 'junior' is in no way a derogatory reflection on the individual's experience. However, some barristers/advocates decide after 10 or 15 years in practice to apply to be allowed to become a Queen's Counsel (QC), also called Leading Counsel or 'silks' in England and Wales and Northern Ireland, and Senior Counsel in Scotland. The application in England and Wales is made to the Lord Chancellor; in Scotland to the Lord Justice General; and in Northern Ireland to the Lord Chief Justice. Applications are considered on the basis of the applicant's proven ability during his or her career, bearing in mind the number of QCs already practising in the applicant's particular branch of the law. A balance has to be kept between the number of juniors and QCs working in different fields, as the nature of the work they undertake, and the fees they are paid, are different.

Having 'taken silk' (the expression arising from the fact that QCs are entitled to wear silk gowns), the QCs' fees are increased by about two-thirds and they become engaged principally in advising and court appearances. Junior counsel are usually engaged to assist QCs since barristers generally stop settling pleadings (that is, drafting the formal written statements which set out a party's case) after taking silk.

When a client goes to a QC, he or she is sure of obtaining the advice of an acknowledged expert in a particular branch of the law. Taking silk will help to confirm the reputation of a barrister/advocate, but the competition for work of the appropriate quality will be intense. Initially, because of the drop in the amount of work coming in, the QC may earn less than a busy junior.

## The Range of Work

As with solicitors, there is a wide range of work to choose from as a barrister/advocate. In Scotland, advocates tend to be less specialised and have to be prepared to deal with the very wide range of cases that are referred to them. This is also true of the practices of many barristers in England and Wales and Northern Ireland but, particularly in London, there are specialist chambers in which all the barristers are engaged almost exclusively in cases in one area of the law, such as chancery work or building cases or copyright matters. Barristers in specialist chambers often find it takes longer to build up a practice, but in the end the rewards can be greater. If you start work in criminal chambers, because there is a large amount of work available in that field it usually means that you will start to earn more at an earlier stage. As you are studying you should try to work out which areas of the law interest you particularly, and whether you are the sort of person who prefers to be in court every day dealing with a mixed bag of cases that might affect any individual, or whether you prefer to deal with large commercial matters which will involve you in research and bring you into contact with clients who are probably quite well versed in their field.

If you choose to become a barrister/advocate you are likely to find the work very satisfying, if at first a little hair-raising. All young barristers/advocates have tales of going to court, and the judge and their opponents having long discussions about a clearly relevant case or section of a statute that they themselves have never even heard of! But for all that, and despite the initial financial instability and competition for jobs, it is quite clear that many really love the work they do.

## Earnings

It is virtually impossible to give any clear indication of what you could earn as a barrister/advocate because the range of incomes is enormous. As a broad generalisation, in London a barrister of five to nine years' call might currently expect to earn at least £25,000 and perhaps much more. In the provinces, the comparable figures might be 10 per cent less, but again one must emphasise that a great deal depends upon the ability and reputation of the individual concerned.

*Case Studies*
Karen

Karen was called to the Bar seven years ago. A member of Gray's Inn, she taught law for five years before starting pupillage, and is now a tenant in a set of chambers in the Temple in London. Most of the barristers in her chambers have a general common law practice, covering both civil and criminal cases, but her particular areas of interest are immigration, employment, personal injury, landlord and tenant, and other housing matters.

It is easy to forget how all at sea you felt when you started in practice, yet some of my first impressions relate to things which I now take for granted. I remember the first time I went to court with my pupil master in the first six months of my pupillage. I was very excited at the prospect. My clearest recollection of my first day in court has nothing to do with the law or the facts of the case. What I remember is that my wig felt uncomfortable, my gown was too long, and my collar was too tight!

You get used to having to wear black, in time, and you learn what clothes look neat and feel comfortable with the formal collar and gown – you also get used to your career being incompatible with an ordered social life! In the second six months as a pupil you 'get on your feet' and can represent clients in court. Again, I remember my first brief, not so much for the case itself as for the surrounding circumstances. It was in the summer and I had been hanging around chambers for a couple of days hoping that the clerk might give me a brief. Finally, on a particularly lovely afternoon, I decided to give up my vigil and go and play tennis, and I had just made all the arrangements when the clerk told me I could go to court instead if I wanted to! Faced with the prospect of my first case, the game went by the board. I soon realised why barristers never make firm social commitments midweek. You can never be sure that you won't have to work in an evening, and, if you take on criminal cases, you have the added problem that the Crown Courts, except in particularly complex or lengthy cases, do not publish the lists of the cases they will hear the next day until about 4 pm on the afternoon before. So it is not until that time that you know whether you will be in court, or where. If you are in court you will probably need to spend the evening reading the papers. Of course, no matter how inconvenient this may be, no barrister, particularly one starting at the Bar, will ever want to turn work away. It has not been unknown for me to go the the theatre and leave at the first interval to go and work on papers for the next day. To have a career at the Bar you have to be prepared to arrange the rest of your life around it and you have to enjoy what you are doing enough not to resent that.

When I started, like many barristers in common law chambers I was given a lot of criminal cases, although I was not defending rapists and murderers in the Old Bailey and obtaining their acquittal by brilliant displays of my forensic skills! When you start, you'll be in the magistrates' courts dealing with people accused of shoplifting; driving offences; minor robberies, burglaries and juvenile crime. It is unlikely that you will start by defending hard-fought cases. You will probably be making applications for bail for your clients or representing them at committal or remand hearings, or simply making pleas in mitigation on their behalf in cases where they have pleaded guilty to the charge. At about the time you start dealing with 'fights' in the magistrates' courts you will probably start receiving briefs to undertake the smaller matters in the Crown Courts.

Equally, if you start with civil cases you won't be dealing with contested divorces or High Court disputes over defectively built public buildings, but you may appear in magistrates' courts representing wives in undefended claims for maintenance from their husbands, and you will often be asked to advise on smaller consumer problems. As your experience grows, so will the level of responsibility and you will soon have the opportunity to take on a variety of county court cases such as disputes between landlords and tenants; parents over children; buyers and sellers over products or payments.

Apart from the actual appearances in court and the style of life, just finding your way around can be a bit daunting at first. I learned early on that it was very easy to miss meals, and so my advice to anyone starting out is, like the condemned man, eat a hearty breakfast!

As I have indicated, your first briefs will probably take you to one of the many magistrates' courts; therefore your first problem of the day could be finding the court so as to arrive there at least half an hour before the magistrates start sitting. This usually means arriving at about 10 am, although, just to confuse the beginner, some start hearing cases as early as 9.30 am. Quite often in small legally aided cases the solicitors won't send a representative along, so once at court the next task is to find your client, which is not always easy if you have never met the person and the court is crowded. Having found your client you take instructions, find your opponent, sign the courts list and, nine times out of ten, wait.

The organisation of courts is much like that of the average GP's surgery, where several people are told to come at the same time on the basis that some will never turn up at all and those who do will not all need as long to be treated as has been set aside for them. The result is also the same – a lot of people end up waiting. This is something you just have to accept when you start going to court, particularly in the early days when you are dealing with smaller cases. Often you will be briefed to appear in several cases at the same court in one day, and inevitably the day will come when your cases do not run consecutively but are listed to take place all at the same time in different court rooms – that is when you learn tact in placating tribunals! After a day in court you have to go back to chambers, report to your instructing solicitors on the day's cases and, if necessary, start work on the next day's papers. When you finally get home, you must eat!

The way your practice builds up, and the success you achieve, is largely dependent on your clerk. It is the clerk who persuades a solicitor to try you out and who assesses when you are ready to take on more difficult cases. A good clerk will build up not only your practice, but also your confidence to match it. Slowly you will start to specialise to some extent, since it is extremely difficult to keep abreast of developments in the law right across the board, and also your clients will look to you not only to advise them on their legal position but to give a prediction of what is likely to happen to them. It is not much use telling a client accused of dangerous driving that the maximum penalty is two years' imprisonment when, owing to the circumstances of the case, the court is likely to hand down a fine. This is the sort of knowledge that you can only gain by practical experience, and so many barristers do specialise.

Personally, I chose to give up matrimonial cases as it would no longer be cost-effective for me to spare the time I would need to spend in preparation to feel confident with these sorts of cases.

As with other careers there are frustrations. It is annoying when you have spent hours preparing for a case and the client does not turn up at court, or the court does not have time to hear the case that day. It is certainly not easy to get started at the Bar, and you have to wait so long to be paid for the work you have done. If you are a woman, or were educated at a comprehensive school, or obtained your degree at a polytechnic, you will find yourself in the minority, and you may find getting started more difficult without money or contacts. Although the Bar is still predominantly a profession for the middle-class male, the old barriers are breaking down, and with the availability of grants and loans you should make a living if you are bright enough and sufficiently committed. The benefits of a career at the Bar, in my view, far outweigh the disadvantages. It is one of the few jobs where you can be sure that the job will grow with you. As you become more able you can take on more work and more demanding cases. You also have the power to set your own hours, though that freedom is usually the freedom to work all hours God sends. But you do retain the final choice in what you do. There is also the great excitment of the job – both the mental stimulation and the unashamed theatrical buzz. There are times in court when I am arguing difficult points of law with an equally able opponent and an interested judge, and I realise that this is what I really want to be doing.

Richard

Richard was called 10 years ago. He is a tenant in a set of chambers in the Temple in London, which he shares with five QCs and about 20 other barristers, all of whom undertake a range of general common law work. His cases are both civil (such as commercial disputes, landlord and tenant problems, personal injury claims and matrimonial work) and criminal (of all types). His work load is split about evenly between civil and criminal matters.

The best way I can describe my job is to outline a fairly typical week:

*Sunday*: After dinner at about 8 pm I did some preparation on the brief I had for the next morning and worked until midnight. It is quite normal for me to have to work at weekends, especially between October and July. The courts take a summer break, and when term starts in the autumn I manage to keep abreast of things during the week, but as Christmas approaches and I spend more time in court and become progressively more tired, I have to start working at weekends to keep up.

*Monday*: At 7 am I got up and drove to Maidstone Crown Court and was in court from 10 am to 12.30 pm, opposing an appeal against conviction by a man convicted of dangerous driving. His application was unsuccessful. The case finished early so I decided to take a long lunch break, and was back in chambers around 4 pm. I then drafted a pleading in a civil case I had been instructed in, and at 5 pm three briefs for the following day were delivered to me. I worked on these until 6.30 pm and then went home. After dinner I did a further hour-and-a-half's work on the briefs.

*Tuesday*: I was up again at 7 am and caught the 8.35 train from Liverpool Street to Cambridge, arriving at court by 10 am. The three briefs were to appear as prosecuting counsel to oppose appeals against sentence that were being brought by three people, two convicted of causing actual bodily harm, and the other of a motoring offence. I had read the papers on the train and discused the cases with my instructing solicitors for half an hour, and I was then in court from 10.30 am to 12.30 pm, and from 1.30 pm to 4.30 pm. My clerk told me I was to be back in Cambridge again next day and that the briefs were in chambers, so I went back to London and picked up the papers at about 7 pm and went home. I should have read the briefs that night but as I didn't get home until 8 p.m, I confess that after dinner I fell asleep in an armchair at about 9 pm!

*Wednesday*: I took the same train to Cambridge, reading the papers on the way. This time I was to prosecute a shoplifter, and oppose the appeal against conviction of a man found guilty of stealing from his employer. I was in court the whole day and returned to chambers to collect Thursday's papers. I worked on these for an hour and then went home where I did a further three hours' work finishing around midnight.

*Thursday*: I caught the 8.10 am train from Victoria to Canterbury, arriving before 10 am, having gone over the papers on the train. I had been briefed in a civil case in which I was defending a man whose landlord was trying to evict him. The case proved to be too long to be heard in the time the court had set aside for it, so it was adjourned, part-heard, at lunch-time. I went back to chambers and worked on a set of civil papers. I had been instructed to advise in a contractual matter and to settle pleadings if I felt it was an appropriate case to fight. I was home by 8 pm.

*Friday*: I was in chambers all day working on papers. I try to return paperwork to solicitors in about a fortnight, and it certainly helps if I can have an uninterrupted day once in a while. Without that I have to work on papers after court and at weekends. That day I worked until 7 pm.

While it is true that barristers earn above average income, it must be clear from the outline of my week that no one joins the profession just for the money, and if you took the hourly rate for the job it is obvious that you could earn a lot more doing something else requiring a similar level of responsibility and skill. What I enjoy is the control I have over what I do – on Monday I took a long lunch break and as a result I had to work late, but that was my choice and I didn't have to explain it to anyone.

To succeed at the Bar you have to be prepared to work hard, and as the law will take up so much of your life you will really have to be dedicated. It helps to be self-critical and you will find it useful to develop a short-term memory, so that you can remember all the details of a case precisely for as long as you need to and then be able to forget them again and clear your mind for the next case. And even if you are normally a shy person in your private life, to succeed at the Bar you will have to become something of an actor. To help your client you will have to learn your part and be able to put it over well.

# Chapter 4

# Other Jobs for the Legally Qualified

## Introduction

Not everyone who qualifies as a solicitor or a barrister/advocate wants to work in private practice. Once you have the basic professional qualifications there is a wide range of careers open to you which will employ the skills you have acquired.

Many qualified lawyers work outside the legal profession altogether. Politics, publishing and management all attract their fair share of lawyers, but even if you want to continue working in the law you may still prefer to do so in a different environment from that in which you were trained. Industry, government and a variety of charities and government-funded bodies employ an increasing number of legal staff. There are also some vacancies for legal executives and solicitors' clerks in these fields (see Chapter 5).

The attraction of these jobs is often the fringe benefits that go with them in terms of pensions, longer holidays, a defined career structure and the prospect of more regular working hours. This is not to imply that these jobs are an easy option – many are as demanding as private practice – and with the increase in the number of people qualifying on both sides of the profession the competition for these vacancies has increased as well.

The following are some examples of jobs outside private practice. The list is not exhaustive, so if you are interested keep an eye out for advertisements in the press and contact any organisations that you would like to work for, as many charities, pressure groups and government agencies employ lawyers.

## The Civil Service

Over 1,000 solicitors, barristers and advocates are employed by UK central government and they make a substantial contribution to a wide range of necessary services.

While some lawyers in the Civil Service are employed in work similar to that in private practice, including litigation and conveyancing, others do the sort of work which they would otherwise never come across, such as dealing with administrative and constitutional problems. Some work directly for the Crown (in the Customs and Excise, for example) whereas others are engaged in work which directly benefits the community (such as for the Charity Commission).

There are some 20 main departments which you might consider joining including the Foreign and Commonwealth Office, the Department of Trade and Industry, the Office of Fair Trading, the Inland Revenue, the Land Registry, HM Customs and Excise, the Lord Advocate's Department and the Lord Chancellor's Department.

Most staff are recruited through the Civil Service Commission at Alencon Link (see p 122) but there are many schemes for recruitment held throughout the year for posts all over the United Kingdom and these vacancies are advertised both in the national press and in professional journals. Information relating to Civil Service jobs in Northern Ireland can also be obtained from the Civil Service Commission in Belfast (see p 116).

## The Prosecution Service

In all three jurisdictions, criminal prosecutions are now conducted on behalf of the State through lawyers employed by the government.

The Prosecution of Offences Act 1985 established in England and Wales for the first time a Crown prosecution service which from 1 April 1986 took over responsibility for prosecutions (except for the very minor motoring offences known as 'specified proceedings') which had previously been undertaken by the police. Since the creation of the Crown prosecution service the job of the police has been restricted to that of investigating crime. It is the job of the legally qualified prosecutors to decide which cases should come to court and to present the prosecution's case in court. The head of the service in England and Wales is the Director of Public Prosecutions and under him are some 2,000 prosecutors employed in branch offices countrywide. The purpose of the system is to ensure greater consistency in prosecuting practice throughout the country. Further information is available from the service's Recruitment Branch at 4–12 Queen Anne's Gate, London SW1H 9TZ.

In Scotland, the Crown Office (see p 122), headed by the Crown Agent, organises and controls the Procurator Fiscal Service. Scotland has a tradition of prosecutions being undertaken independently of the police force through the procurators fiscal who are responsible for prosecutions in the sheriff and district courts. There are about 50 procurators fiscal who are employed throughout Scotland to investigate crimes and to institute criminal proceedings within their court's district and who also present the cases in court in a similar way to the Crown prosecutors in England and Wales. The more serious offences in the High Court are prosecuted by the Crown Office.

In Northern Ireland, as in England and Wales, prosecutions are undertaken by the Director of Public Prosecutions, whose staff are legally qualified.

## Local Government

Local authorities throughout the UK employ many lawyers for a wide range of work. Some of their work, like that of civil servants, is akin to that carried on in private practice, such as conveyancing, planning and litigation, but even here the nature of the cases will be specialised – rather than buying and selling private homes, they may be in charge of letting or selling council houses; the planning might involve local road construction or industrial development. Equally, some work will be peculiar to local government – lawyers will often be involved in public inquiries; assisting the social services with, for example, child care proceedings; and they also undertake personnel work for the council. Often, lawyers doing this sort of work will have decided on a job in local government early in their careers and will have specialised in their training accordingly, often having served articles or completed the post-CPE training contract with a local government department. This is not essential, and you might choose to work for a local authority having completed your training and obtained experience in private practice.

Jobs in local government are advertised in the national press and professional journals, and you could try applying direct to the local authorities in the areas in which you would like to work.

## Magistrates' Courts Service

Magistrates' courts in England and Wales deal with 98 per cent of all criminal cases and have jurisdiction in respect of domestic, juvenile and licensing business. There are approximately 27,800 lay unpaid magistrates (justices of the peace) and 61 stipendiary magistrates (47 in London and 14 in the provinces) who are legally qualified and salaried. While the lay magistrates are given training for their work, they require the assistance of a legally qualified court clerk to assist them in their understanding of the law when reaching their decisions.

Justices' clerks advise the lay magistrates on law, practice and procedure and are also responsible for the administration of the local magistrates' courts service. There are 288 justices' clerks and 9,000 members of staff in the magistrates' courts service. A justices' clerk must be a solicitor or barrister of at least five years' standing with experience in a justices' clerk's office.

Apart from the justices' clerk, the magistrates' courts service employs a considerable number of solicitors and barristers, many of whom receive their training as such while serving as trainees in the service, although others obtain these qualifications beforehand. Appropriate leave and financial assistance is usually provided to enable trainees to qualify as solicitors or barristers.

In order to progress in the court service it may be necessary to move from one area to another, both to gain experience and to take posts with greater responsibilities and consequently higher salaries. Justices' clerks' salaries vary with the size of the community their courts serve, and details of pay can be obtained from C2 Division of the Home Office (see p 123). With the job goes a contributory pension scheme and a minimum of five weeks' holiday per year.

In Scotland, District courts are administered by local authorities. Clerks in the Scottish Court Service are non-legal staff at the court of session, the High Court of Justiciary and the sheriff court.

In Northern Ireland there are no lay magistrates, and there is therefore no equivalent to the office of justices' clerk.

## Industry and Commerce

Industrial and commercial institutions, public bodies, and business organisations of all kinds employ lawyers. Indeed, the majority of barristers called each year do not go into private practice; many of them are attracted by the potentially greater security of a career in business. If you go to work in industry the areas of law you will deal with will depend on the nature of the organisation that you join. If your employer is a retailer, whether marketing pharmaceuticals, cars or high fashion, you will undoubtedly need to advise on consumer legislation; if your employer exports anything from books to bottled beer you will have to explain the requirements of international and EC law, and help resolve disputes over shipping agreements and the carriage of the goods. Manufacturing companies, buying raw materials and selling finished products, will require advice on contracts entered into, and assistance in arguments arising out of, say, the non-delivery of materials and the non-acceptance of goods. Lawyers in property companies become involved in conveyancing, landlord and tenant cases, and building projects. Financial institutions, banks and insurance houses need lawyers who know about tax and general company and commercial matters, and most companies will require you to have a knowledge of company law and employment law. In all cases you are likely to become involved with problems at a much earlier stage than you would in private practice, which can make the job more interesting and constructive. The Bar Association for Commerce, Finance and Industry (BACFI) publishes a useful booklet, *Barristers In Business*, which provides a picture of the work that in-house barristers do.

Although it is difficult to generalise about the type of job you could find yourself doing, to succeed in the business world you are going to need commercial sense and an ability to find practical solutions as well as legal answers. As your employer will also be your client, you will need to be able to react quickly to situations as they arise, and as your input will only be part of the equation you will probably be called upon to work alongside other professionals, such as accountants, personnel officers, financial advisers and marketing directors, to resolve problems.

If you are thinking of a career in industry you should consider very carefully where your interests lie, and then try to find out as much as possible about the workings of the organisations to which you intend to apply. Vacancies in industry are advertised in *The Law Society's Gazette*, the *Journal of the Law Society of Scotland*, and in the Inns of Court. In addition, companies advertise in the national press, and BACFI circulates details to members (see p 122). Some employers also recruit through employment agencies, and the firm of Chambers and Partners specialise in the recruitment of lawyers for industry (see p 122).

Work in industry could take you anywhere in the UK, for although in the past large companies have tended to base themselves in cities, there has been a considerable decentralisation in recent years and head offices are now to be found throughout the provinces.

Remuneration in industry tends to involve a package of salary and benefits, such as a company car, a pension scheme, bonuses and possibly subsidised mortgages and loans. As a result the overall remuneration tends to be higher in this type of job than in a similar position in private practice.

*Case Study*
Graham

Graham is a solicitor who went to work in the legal department of a construction company five years after he qualified in private practice. The company employs five solicitors, a barrister, two legal executives and an articled clerk, who between them carry out the company's conveyancing, litigation and debt collecting, as well as advising on company and commercial matters. Graham deals mainly with litigation and commercial work.

The size and organisation of legal departments in industry vary considerably, I don't have the same case-load I had in private practice, but I have to be prepared to advise on the spot in a way I don't think solicitors in private practice are often called on to do. It is impossible to keep the client at arm's length in this job – when the phone rings I cannot put the caller on to my secretary, and if a problem crops up I have to go to meetings at a moment's notice. It is important to be able to think quickly: people contact you when they need rapid decisions and you don't usually get the chance to go away and think about your advice. It is difficult to categorise the major part of my work in terms of legal areas – often I am giving general commercial advice from a legal standpoint.

I find the work I do now much more satisfying than the work I was doing in private practice. I get involved with management at a much earlier stage in the decision-making process, and I hope this means I can prevent problems arising. I also have the opportunity of influencing policy and sometimes of making changes in the company's practices in order to prevent legal difficulties arising in the future. I prefer this direct involvement in a company's affairs to being called in at a much later stage, when all a lawyer can do is clear up the mess!

There are fringe benefits with the job. I have a company car, and because of the nature of the company's business I get some trips abroad. I also travel in the UK quite extensively. I suppose I get away from the office every other week for a day or two. Otherwise my job is probably more nine-to-five-ish than most solicitors'.

## Law Centres

The first Law Centre was set up in 1970 in North Kensington in London and now there are nearly 60 throughout the country, particularly in deprived inner-city areas. They grew up initially in response to local needs for free legal advice and representation for individuals and groups, and they still serve these needs. Law Centres are not sufficiently resourced to work with all the people that come to them; they concentrate on those areas in which they see the greatest local need. Some of the most common areas of work are: housing (eg tenants rights) and homelessness, welfare rights, employment (eg industrial tribunals), planning and environment, children's rights, juvenile crime, education and anti-discrimination work. Some Law Centres also provide a 24-hour emergency service covering detentions by the police, deportations, domestic violence and action against unlawful evictions.

Law Centres consciously make the legal processes and systems less obscure to people. They employ not only legally qualified people but also expert advice workers and community workers to ensure a more welcoming and less intimidating style of work. Law Centres are responsive to the needs of the people within their communities; they help, advise and represent people in a number of ways. This includes development work, such as enabling community-based groups to start up in response to a legal issue in the local area and carrying out case-work for groups of individuals with the same problem. They offer training and education, eg taking in students and volunteers from the local area. Law Centres also carry out research and respond to proposals put forward by government, local authorities or other bodies that affect people in the local area, or that are issues of public interest.

Law Centres are accountable to their local communities and are run by a locally elected management committee, made up of interested individuals and organisations from the area. Management committees are voluntary and members give their time free; they may also have representatives from the local Law Society. All Law Centres are non-profit making. Most are funded by their local authority although a few have grant aid from the Legal Aid Board. Many are increasingly having to rely on legal aid income and support from charities. The Law Centres Federation, which represents Law Centres, would like funding for the Centres to be secure and to be funded nationally. It is also asking for funds for the many new Centres which would like to open.

Jobs in Law Centres are advertised in the national press and in the *Legal Action Group Bulletin* as well as in specialist journals. Information about work in a Law Centre can be obtained from the Law Centres Federation.

*Case Study*
Elaine

Elaine left university with an arts degree and then worked voluntarily as a worker in a law centre. She became so interested in the work that she decided to train as a solicitor with the intention of working in a law centre as soon as she was qualified.

> I am employed to work 35 hours a week and I probably do about that, but I have to be flexible and be available for evening meetings.
>
> A typical week for me probably involves one or two evening meetings with local groups, such as Women's Aid or a tenants' association or our own management committee. In addition, we have staff meetings each week to organise the day-to-day running of the centre. I work on projects and I also see clients by appointment about two half-days a week; the rest of the time is taken up with working on cases.
>
> I really enjoy the work I do, which I find both worthwhile and stimulating. I prefer the flexibility and informality of the law centre, even though I earn less than I could in private practice and jobs in law centres tend to be insecure – they only last as long as their funds, which can be cut at any time.

## Citizens Advice Bureaux

Citizens Advice Bureaux (CABs) were opened after the war to assist members of the public who were in need of help or disoriented as a result of their experiences. Most large towns now have a CAB, funded partly by local government and partly by central government and charities. There are at present 1,012 CABs in England and Wales, 64 in Scotland and 29 in Northern Ireland.

A very small number of CABs in England and Wales employ their own lawyers, both to act as specialist advisers to the rest of the team and also to undertake their own cases on behalf of the bureau's clients. CAB community lawyers are usually solicitors, although barristers have also been employed. The type of case they will see depends on the locality in which the bureau is situated. If the bureau is in a middle-class suburb it is likely that the community lawyer will tend to deal with neighbour disputes and consumer problems, whereas if the bureau is in a deprived inner-city area it is likely that the community lawyer will be involved with such problems as social welfare law, employment, housing and immigration. The policy of CABs is to respond to the needs of the community as they arise.

Unfortunately, CABs and many other advice agencies are at present facing difficulties over funding, but if you are interested in considering this area of work you should contact your local CAB, or the Greater London CAB Service (for London) or the National Association of CAB (for England and Wales), or Citizens Advice Scotland or the Northern Ireland Association of CAB (see pp 122–4).

All CABs in Northern Ireland, and many others throughout the UK, rely on lawyers giving help on a voluntary basis and you might find it interesting to attend voluntary sessions to find out whether the work would appeal to you, or simply to be of help to the community.

## Coroners

Coroners in England and Wales are appointed by local government, and those who are qualified to apply for appointment are barristers, solicitors or legally qualified doctors of five years' standing. In addition to the coroners who serve a local community, all High Court judges are automatically made coroners for the whole of the country.

The job of the coroner is to inquire into deaths occurring within the area in which he serves, where the deceased is known to have died violently, unnaturally, in prison or unexpectedly, or where the cause of death is unknown. A coroner can order a *post mortem* examination and, where necessary, an inquest. Inquests are held in the coroner's court, which considers the evidence concerning the cause of death. The inquest may be heard by the coroner alone or by the coroner and a jury. In either case the court has to return a verdict and certify its findings. It is no longer the coroner's job to suggest who may be guilty if the verdict is one of murder, manslaughter or infanticide, and it is now left to the police to follow up such possible charges. Coroners also lead investigations into the finding of treasure-trove!

In Scotland the job of the coroner is undertaken by the procurators fiscal. In Northern Ireland coroners must be practising barristers or solicitors of not less than five years' standing.

## Licensed Conveyancers

The profession of licensed conveyancers was created as recently as 11 May 1987. Licensed conveyancers are men and women who are legally qualified to advise on all aspects of the transfer of rights to land and property. A degree is not required; every would-be licensed conveyancer applies for registration as a student with the Council for Licensed Conveyancers. The basic educational requirement is four O levels or equivalent including English, but mature students may be accepted on the basis of their experience alone. Having registered, a student must pass the Council's examinations and fulfil a practical training requirement. Part I of the examination is of A level standard; Part II deals with areas of law, practice and accounting which are relevant to conveyancing. Exams are held twice a year. Most students attend part-time courses run at colleges throughout the country. Correspondence courses are also available. Further information is available from the Council's Education Officer (see p 122).

# Chapter 5

# Legal Executives

## Introduction

Solicitors throughout the UK have traditionally employed non-qualified personnel to assist them with their legal work. In the nineteenth century solicitors had many clerks, most of whom were engaged in secretarial functions such as drawing up and copying legal documents. However, there have always been some senior clerks who had a legal rather than clerical function. These 'managing clerks' tended to specialise in particular areas of law and undertook considerable responsibility for day-to-day running of cases under the supervision of their principals.

Today most firms in England and Wales employ non-qualified staff to help with legal work and at present there are thought to be some 22,000 clerks working in private practice. In Northern Ireland non-qualified legal assistants are called law clerks, but their numbers are steadily dwindling and work which was traditionally undertaken by law clerks in Northern Ireland is now more often undertaken by trainees and qualified assistant solicitors, and in Scotland the pattern is similar.

In all three jurisdictions it is possible to join a solicitors' firm straight from school without any specific qualifications and start work as a clerk, learning the job from experience and informal tuition given in the course of employment by the solicitor employer. However, the Institute of Legal Executives (see p 123) was set up in England and Wales with the support of the Law Society in 1963, and this provides a recognised system of formal training and exams for such employment. The Institute also attempts to protect the status and interests of its members while improving the quality of recruits. The Institute currently has some 21,000 members most of whom are in England and Wales, but some law clerks in Northern Ireland are also members, having prepared for the exam by correspondence course.

Strictly speaking the title 'Legal Executive' should only be applied to Fellows of the Institute, but the expression has come to be used much more generally and is often applied to any assistants who are not solicitors, though some refer to themselves by the older title of managing clerk, or solicitors' clerk, or even manager or clerk. It may be that a scheme similar to that provided by the Institute will be set up in Scotland or Northern Ireland, but at present there are no formal organisations for legal executives in those two jurisdictions.

## Enrolling as a Student with the Institute

To enrol as a student with the Institute of Legal Executives you will need to have at least four GCSE passes at grades A, B or C. The subjects must include English language, English literature or English, and other passes must be drawn from a list of approved subjects provided by the Institute. Passes in only three approved GCSE subjects will be accepted, provided English is included and at least two of the subjects have been passed at A level. The Institute may also accept other public examinations as evidence that a satisfactory educational level has been reached and, in the case of prospective students over the age of 25, the Institute may waive the basic educational requirement if it is considered that the individual has sufficient professional, business, commercial, academic or other experience. The Institute also now offers a Preliminary Certificate in Legal Studies, as an alternative to GCSEs, for those who cannot meet the minimum educational requirement, or who want some introductory legal studies.

## Training

Full details of the training requirements may be obtained from the Institute of Legal Executives (see p 123). Basically the Institute has three categories of member under the current scheme, namely students, members, and Fellows. You can enrol as a student and take the Membership Examination, and upon passing that, you may become a member of the Institute and thereafter a Fellow.

As a student you will have to prepare for the Membership Examination which is taken in two parts. Part one is equivalent to A level standard and covers an introduction to the legal system plus a basic course in law and procedure. It is possible to study for the part one examination by attending college on a part-time basis or through studying at home with the aid of a correspondence course which is available through Ilex Tutorial Services (see p 123). Some colleges run full-time courses leading to the part one examination, but normally students study over a two-year period while already employed in a solicitors' office or department.

Part two of the Membership Examination is equivalent in standard to a degree, and for it you have to choose one paper in legal practice out of a choice of six (namely, civil litigation, criminal litigation, matrimonial practice, company practice, probate practice, and conveyancing). You must then also pass one paper in substantive law which is directly linked to your choice of practice paper, plus two other papers in substantive law in accordance with the regulations of the Institute, which ensure that these two papers are also linked to the practice paper. The effect of this is to ensure that you obtain specialised knowledge in one major area of solicitors' work.

You can study for the part two examination part time over two or three years, and exams are held at regional centres in the summer and the autumn of each year. Details of centres can be obtained from the Institute.

The difference between the legal executives' Membership Examinations and the solicitors' Final Examinations is that while the standards are equivalent, the number of papers to be taken by the student of the Institute is less, and in addition there is no limit placed on the number of times papers can be attempted. So, if you are interested in this type of work but do not feel you can undertake the solicitors' training, this alternative may well suit you. Once you are qualified as a legal executive, it is always open to you to take advantage of the exemptions given by the Law Society and go on to become a solicitor (see Chapter 2). Indeed, from 1993, the legal executive training scheme will be the main route to qualification as a solicitor for non-graduates.

Students who pass parts one and two of the Membership Examination may apply to be enrolled as members of the Institute. It is not necessary to be in qualifying employment (that is, working in a solicitor's office or a legal department) to take the Membership Examination and qualify for Membership. However, most students are in such work when they start studying, and it is usual to have found employment before starting part two subjects, at the latest.

Once you have qualified as a member, provided you are aged 25 or over and have completed five years in qualifying employment, including two consecutive years as a qualified member, it is possible to apply for admission as a Fellow. Applications for enrolment as a

Fellow have to be supported by a certificate of fitness signed by a partner or senior solicitor of the practice or department in which the applicant is employed.

## How to Find a Job

There is no simple way to find a job. The Law Society has an employment register and some commercial agencies specialise in legal staff; however, a prospective trainee with no previous experience will need to contact solicitors' firms direct, with a carefully prepared C.V.

Advertisements are placed by firms in the *Legal Executive Magazine* (which caters for students, members and Fellows of the Institute), *The Law Society's Gazette*, the *Journal of the Law Society of Scotland* and the national press in all three jurisdictions. Advertisements are also occasionally carried by other legal magazines (see p 119). As in the case of trainee solicitors and solicitors, many jobs come through personal contacts or friends in the profession. Not all solicitors' clerks work in private practice; there are some openings for them in industry and commerce, in local authorities, and in the courts and prosecution services (see Chapter 4).

## The Job

While standards required by part two of the Membership Examination are broadly equivalent to those of the solicitors' Final Examination, the range of subjects is narrower and solicitors' clerks, whether members of the Institute or not, tend to specialise in the type of work they undertake. They are often employed in departments where the procedural aspects of the work are central, as for example in personal injury work, divorce, probate and trusts, debt collecting, and conveyancing.

## Prospects

As a solicitor's clerk, whether a member of the Institute or otherwise, there will always be a limit on what you can do independently. You will not have such an extensive right to represent clients in court as solicitors have, and you will not be able to set up in practice on your own, or become a partner in a firm.

With the increase in the number of solicitors qualifying, some firms may tend to employ young solicitors rather than clerks. This is already happening to a great extent in Northern Ireland and Scotland, and in England and Wales it is likely that those clerks who do not choose to study for the Institute exams will, in future, find it more difficult to gain experience and promotion. However, many firms in England and Wales prefer to employ clerks for certain types of work, since the fact that they tend to specialise means they develop a very useful in-depth knowledge of their own area of the law. In addition, firms may realistically expect that clerks will stay longer in one job as there is not the pressure on them to move to find partnership prospects.

Although as a clerk you will always be working for a solicitor, more experienced clerks work with a minimum of supervision, and handle their own cases. They sometimes manage their own departments, and they have contact with clients in just the same way as solicitors do. Many find that being a solicitor's clerk is a satisfying and stimulating job.

## Salary

Earnings vary with age, geographical area, the type of work specialised in, and the level of responsibility. Typical salary levels for school leavers in 1991 were between £5,000 and £8,000; students aged 21 years of age who have passed part one of the Membership Examinations should receive between £8,000 and £12,000; and Fellows should expect to receive between £16,000 and £20,000. The Institute of Legal Executives quotes examples of qualified and very experienced Fellows receiving salaries in excess of £25,000. Clerks who are not members of the Institute will probably be paid within similar salary ranges, though they will tend to be paid on the basis of their value to the firm rather than any formal qualifications.

*Case Studies*
Michael

Michael works for a seven-partner firm in central London, where he has been for the last 15 years. The department he is in consists of two partners, himself and another legal executive, each of whom has his own assistants and case-load.

I started work in a solicitor's office 30 years ago, and my first job was as a general office clerk. I became interested in law and worked my way up, through outdoor clerk (see pp 108–9) and trainee manager, and in time I took the exams to become a Fellow of the Institute of Legal Executives. I am now in charge of my own section of the department, and with the help of an assistant I handle about 650 current files. The case-load in this type of work is always heavy, but it also brings a lot of contact with clients which goes to make the job both satisfying and interesting.

Many of my clients are referred to the firm through their unions after suffering injuries at work, though I deal with some other accident cases, resulting from road accidents for example. With personal injury cases you could be working on a file from anything between six months and four years, and the clients can be suffering from either minor injuries that will heal completely in time, or such severe injuries that they will never be able to work again.

I usually see all my clients early on, when they are at their worst, so that I can take statements from them while they still remember the details of the accident. As a result, as the case continues I see the progress not only of the legal aspects but also of the client's condition.

As my clients come from all over the country I travel quite a bit more than most lawyers, which I enjoy and which also means that I have a car. Having seen the clients, I take statements from witnesses and then arrange to obtain advice from counsel in more complicated cases, and issue proceedings.

In most workplace accident cases, I end up dealing with employers' insurers and about 90 per cent of my cases are settled before ever coming to court. From that you can gather that an important aspect of my job is negotiating. To be able to settle a case assumes that you are able to show your opponent that in law there can be no dispute about liability, and that all that remains to be agreed is the amount of compensation to be paid. To be confident that your assessment of the settlement sum is correct, you have to develop a good working knowledge of what an injury is 'worth', and that entails keeping up with what the courts are awarding in the cases that do go to trial. You have to be a bit tough to get the amount you believe your client is entitled to, but if you can settle a claim the client will probably get the money sooner, and will avoid legal costs and the strain of a court appearance. Of course, there are cases where, either on liability or on the amount of damages, you just can't reach agreement with the other side, and those cases have to go to trial.

Nowadays not everyone who works as a manager bothers to take the Institute's exams, and, particularly in smaller offices, your employers will not insist on formal qualifications. The advantage of having the exams is that they show a prospective employer that you have reached a level of competence, but many will be just as interested in what experience you have had and where you obtained it. As a legal executive I have a great deal of responsibility for my own work, and possibly as much independence in my work as a solicitor, though it would be true to say that it has taken me longer to reach this level. Possibly it is more difficult to move jobs and keep the same level of pay as a manager or legal executive since, to some extent, your salary is a reflection of how useful you are to a firm.

Basically I enjoy the job: no two cases are ever quite the same. Yet, by specialising in an area of the law, you are able to become highly effective and efficient as you gain in practical experience.

## David

David works for a 20-partner firm in central London, where he has been for seven years. He works in the Family department, which is split into those undertaking trust work and those dealing exclusively with probate. David and another managing clerk (neither of whom has ever taken any of the Institute's exams) specialise in probate under the supervision of a partner.

I went to work in a solicitor's office on leaving school, about 20 years ago. Unlike many managers I didn't start out as an outdoor clerk but started in a trust department dealing with income tax returns. I wanted an office job and I saw this one advertised in the press.

The joke about lawyers doing probate is that all their clients are dead! But, of course, although the work consists of sorting out the estates of people who have died, your clients are the executors under the will or the next of kin, and they are very much alive! If they are near relatives they will need a lot more from you than just your legal expertise. In fact, with this sort of work, you can be sure that you will meet the clients at least a couple of times. They have to come to see you to give you instructions initially, and there are always papers for them to sign and affidavits for them to swear, so they usually come to the office a few times.

I tend to deal with professional executors such as banks and accountants. They usually know almost as much about some aspects of my job as I do, and that helps to keep up my standards.

I enjoy probate work. The estates vary considerably in size from only a few thousand pounds to millions. The size of the estate affects the turnover of the cases. An average uncomplicated estate can be wound up completely in nine months, whereas the larger the assets and the more complicated the provisions of the will, the longer the job can take. I will work on some cases for a number of years.

Probate work tends not to impose its own time limits in the way that litigation does. It is easy to let things slide if you don't have self-discipline and keep to your own work plans. There is a certain amount of mathematics in my job and some people feel put off by that – although I don't mind it. There are always tedious aspects to all jobs, and with mine it is the finishing off of cases which requires the preparation of accounts. The real plus, so far as I am concerned, is that the work I do has a lot of law in it. That may sound a funny thing for a lawyer to say, but many legal jobs involve more procedure than actual law and advising on law. In a probate department you have to understand revenue law, which changes with every Finance Act. To administer estates, and to advise clients on the best way to provide for their relatives on their death, you have to know about inheritance tax, capital gains tax, and income tax, which are likely to alter, against the background of the Administration of Estates Act and the Wills Act which remain the same. You also need to have a working knowledge of conveyancing and company law and litigation.

I have never taken any exams. I have a family and it is very difficult to study in those circumstances. I find I have my work cut out keeping up with changes in the law without setting out to undertake any formal studies. I haven't found the fact that I don't have any of the Institute exams has ever stood in my way. As a managing clerk I feel I could have difficulties in getting another job, and there seems to be no strictly adhered-to salary scales to which one can refer, though at my age employers tend to look at what experience you've had, and which firms you've been with, rather than whether you are a Fellow of the Institute. But I think for young people starting in this career now, exams are more important.

I enjoy my job and I find it mentally challenging, but I wouldn't choose it if I were starting again. Young people going into the legal profession should be aware that it is very class-structured. Traditionally, solicitors came from the middle classes, and their clerks were more likely to be from working-class backgrounds. That division may be less obvious now, with more and more solicitors qualifying from very varied backgrounds. But these attitudes are still prevalent, and if you are not a solicitor you will always be an employee – a clerk can never be one of the bosses.

*Chapter 6*

# Barristers' and Advocates' Clerks

## Clerks in England and Wales

Barristers' clerks in England and Wales constitute a small profession which is almost unknown outside the legal world. They are responsible for the administration of barristers' chambers and for the professional lives of the barristers they serve. The title 'clerk' is now a misnomer, since it does not adequately describe the managerial nature of the role. Possibly 'Executive Manager' would today be a more accurate title for a clerk to chambers.

Each set of chambers has its own individual administrative organisation but they all follow a broadly similar pattern. There is a senior clerk, known as 'the clerk to chambers' who is assisted by the first junior clerk, who acts as his deputy, and by other junior clerks and typists who are employed by the Head of Chambers (a senior barrister – see p 47).

Most barristers' clerks start work in a set of chambers straight from school, as this is very much a profession where you start at the bottom and learn on the job as you move up. Although the pay is not at first exceptional, the profession provides opportunities for those who prove themselves able to make the grade to obtain considerable financial rewards and job satisfaction. A few applicants may have contacts in the field, but the majority will have heard of the job for the first time through local careers offices, who are kept informed of vacancies by the Institute of Barristers' Clerks.

The basic educational requirements for a prospective clerk are four GCSEs at grades A to C, two of which must be English and mathematics. Equivalent qualifications may be accepted.

## Training

New entrants who do not already have high or professional qualifications will take up occupation at a junior level in chambers to undertake practical training. They can apply through the Institute to attend a two-year part-time course of further education under the heading of a BTec National Certificate, studying in the first year Organisation, Finance and Management, and in the second year Law, Marketing and Chambers' Administration.

On obtaining the BTec Certificate, you can apply for qualified membership of the Institute and you will also be eligible to enrol at a university for further qualification if you so wish.

## The Job

The barristers' clerk has to organise the barristers' day. This includes accepting instructions from solicitors; ensuring that written advice given by the barristers is typed and returned to instructing solicitors; arranging conferences for solicitors and their clients with counsel and making sure that any papers the barrister will have to see before advising are received in time for them to be read; checking the lists produced by the various courts to see whether the barristers in that chambers are involved in any cases listed for hearing, and then notifying the barristers and solicitors concerned. An important aspect of the work is that the clerk should establish trust and goodwill with court officials, and the job requires a very high standard of integrity.

Sometimes a barrister will be briefed to appear in two cases that clash, and when that happens the clerk tries to ensure, if the solicitors so require, that another barrister in the chambers can appear instead. A clerk's day is dictated to a large degree by the fact that the courts do not publish lists of the cases to be heard on one day until late afternoon of the day before, and so it is only towards the end of a day that the clerks can try to sort out where the barristers in their chambers will be appearing the next day and sort out any problems arising. Clerks also have to be available at lunch-times so that the barristers who are at court can ring in, either to take messages or to check their appointments. Thus, to succeed as a barristers' clerk you will have to be able to cope with demands being made on you by solicitors and time limits, as well as by the barristers themselves. A clerk's day can never be ordered – the telephone has to be answered and one must be flexible enough to move easily from one job to another without getting flustered or bad tempered. Whatever the problems, clerks have to remain courteous – they are the public relations officers for the chambers, and the extent to which solicitors consider they get good service from the chambers (which depends largely on their relationship with the clerk) may well affect the amount of work they send. To do this job you must be able to work under pressure and be prepared to work long hours and accept responsibility, but the quality most necessary, according to the Institute of Barristers' Clerks, is common sense.

## Prospects

As a school-leaver starting work in chambers you will find you are expected to fill in where needed, however mundane the tasks. Along with accompanying barristers to court and carrying their books and robes from one court to another, you will be expected to run errands – collecting and delivering papers, answering phones, and making tea. For the first couple of years you must expect to be something of a general dogsbody, but as you gain experience and learn about the organisation of the office and the legal system, you will be given specific areas of responsibility to relieve the more senior clerks. You may take over the responsibility of checking the court lists; you will start to accept instructions from solicitors and negotiate fees on behalf of the barristers; you may, as a more experienced junior clerk in chambers, have the job of writing up the diary showing where each barrister is to be on the following day.

It should be stressed that the profession of clerk, like that of barrister, although once an exclusively male domain, has become open to women and there are both senior and junior female clerks.

There are at present about 300 barristers' senior clerks, and approximately 380 junior clerks. A junior clerk may have to move from one set of chambers to another to gain promotion and experience.

When you become a senior clerk your responsibilities will grow. A senior clerk will be concerned principally with the work of the Queen's Counsel in chambers (see p 55). In addition, the senior clerk is also the office manager, welfare officer and father-confessor rolled into one, to both staff and barristers alike. He or she has to make sure, for example, that the building is kept in good repair and that there are adequate funds for the bills to be paid.

## Salary

The Institute makes no recommendations for minimum levels of pay, but you should expect your wages to increase with your experience, and as you take on further responsibilities. It is not unusual for senior clerks to pay a percentage of their own earnings to the more senior of the junior clerks.

Junior clerks are usually paid by the Head of Chambers, but senior clerks are paid by individual barristers, usually by way of a fee which is included in the barrister's own fee and represents a payment by the solicitor to the clerk for his services. The fee is five per cent of the barrister's fee. Some chambers have recently taken up the recommendations of the Royal Commission on Legal Services and offer new senior clerks a salary and a reduced percentage fee, but the Institute favours the traditional form of payment.

*Case Study*
A senior clerk

> I have been a barristers' clerk for 28 years. I started in the Temple in London in a small set of chambers with one QC and four junior barristers, where I was the sole junior clerk with responsibilities that included tea-making and typing. In 1962 I moved to my present chambers as a second junior clerk. I am now the senior clerk, with three juniors to assist me, and together we serve five QCs and 21 barristers.
>
> A clerk's job is an unusual combination – you have to be an administrator, a diplomat and a buffer! To deal with the administrative aspects you have to be very organised and careful in your work. Diplomacy is needed because although you are concerned with the individual practices of each of the barristers in chambers, a good clerk has to bear in mind the long-term good of the chambers as a whole, and to that extent he or she has to balance the convenience and interest of any individual barrister against that. The clerk is the buffer between the barristers and their instructing solicitors; and as well as keeping the barristers happy and working, the clerk has to provide a service to the solicitors. It is the clerk who contributes a lot towards building the solicitors' confidence in the chambers, which means that when the barrister of their choice is not available, the solicitors will ask for the clerk's guidance as to which other junior barrister in the chambers would be able to assist. This is the way in which a lot of young barristers get work; equally, from the solicitors' comments the clerks can learn about the ability of the barristers they serve.
>
> Clerks have a close relationship with the barristers in their chambers. They are usually addressed by their Christian names even by the most

junior pupils, whereas the clerk, on the other hand, always addresses all barristers as 'Sir' or 'Madam'. Yet the senior clerk will, nonetheless, direct the junior barristers, advising on problems of etiquette and procedure and selecting the cases they are offered.

The job cannot be from nine to five. Clerks *have* to work until the day's court work tasks are finished, and the more senior clerks always have to be on call to deal with problems, both personal and professional, as they arise. It is quite common for a lot of paper work to be done at home during the weekend or sometimes, in an emergency, overnight!

A school-leaver will have to get used to the chambers' organisation and the legal system, as well as learning new skills. Computers are now being introduced into chambers, usually for the purpose of fee collection, and will have to be mastered by those who use them. For many, the job of barristers' clerk will be too pressurised. It is a job that needs to be learned from the bottom to the top to ensure thorough competency. An essential ingredient is common sense, together with enjoyment of the challenge of responsibility. It is hard work, but rewarding. You see other people developing their careers and you know you have contributed – and at the same time you are developing your own specialised skills. I wouldn't choose to be doing anything else.

## Clerks in Scotland

In Scotland, advocates do not join together in chambers as they do in England and Wales, but rather work from the Advocates' Library. The Bar in Scotland is divided into nine 'stables' each of which is served by an advocates' clerk and a deputy clerk employed by Faculty Services Limited (see p 123).

The nine clerks as a group are directly supported by nine deputies, who are backed up by clerical and secretarial staff. Faculty Services Limited also employs accounting staff who deal with the issue and collection of the advocates' fees. There is also a typing pool available to deal with the output of the advocates, though a number of them also employ personal secretaries.

The number of advocates' clerks is too small to warrant a formal training programme and training is provided in-service. There are no formal educational standards that have to be established to apply for the job of a clerk, though clearly this is a matter which is taken into consideration when applications are under review.

The number of vacancies as a clerk are relatively few since the clerks constitute a very settled workforce and recruitment has only been necessary to cater for the increasing number of practising advocates.

The job of the advocates' clerk is very similar to that of the barristers' clerk in England and Wales. The clerk is an intermediary between instructing solicitors and counsel, and his responsibility is to ensure that the advocates within his stable receive an appropriate workflow, and to advise solicitors which counsel are suitable and available for any particular case. It should be added, however, that solicitors often send instructions direct to advocates without using the clerk as an intermediary. As in the case of barristers in England and Wales, advocates in Scotland contribute a proportion of their gross earnings towards the payment of their clerks but in Scotland this is arranged by way of the advocates paying to Faculty Services Limited which then pays the employed clerks. The rate of pay for advocates' clerks is linked to the Civil Service scale on a level which roughly relates to a comparable post within the courts' administration.

## Clerks in Northern Ireland

Barristers in Northern Ireland work from the Bar Library of the Royal Courts of Justice, where each has a desk. They do not employ clerks either individually or collectively.

# Chapter 7

# Court Reporters

## Introduction

Court reporters, also known as shorthand writers, attend court
hearings and take a complete verbatim record of the evidence,
the judgments, the summings up and sometimes the speeches of
counsel. They should not be confused with reporting barristers,
who write reports of cases for legal journals, or with newspaper
reporters who write summaries of hearings for the national press.

A record of court proceedings has to be made for two reasons.
A case may be appealed and the appeal court will need an accurate
account of the earlier hearing to see how the lower court reached its
decision. In addition, as longer cases progress, the lawyers involved
often wish to see a transcript of the day's proceedings, to remind
them of the evidence that has been given and to help them prepare
for the next stage of the case.

## England and Wales

In most instances in the High Court and the Crown Courts, where
the major civil and criminal cases are heard, an official record
has to be made of the evidence given by witnesses and of the
judge's summing up and the judgment. The Lord Chancellor
appoints firms to undertake this duty, and their staff – the court
reporters – take a note of the proceedings, currently in shorthand
or with a stenotype machine, although the use of pen shorthand is
being phased out as court centres increasingly move to computer-
aided transcription. Sometimes, court reporters will use a portable
tape recorder to assist them, and some courts have installed tape
recorders as the sole method of taking the record. However the
record is made, it is also the court reporter's job to produce any
typed transcripts which may be required.

Firms which undertake court reporting are also called on to

provide shorthand writers to take notes for conferences and meetings, both public and private, so while you may train and be employed primarily for working within the court system, your skills may involve you in other fields from time to time.

There are no formal educational requirements for joining the profession, but preference is given to those with GCSE and A level passes and shorthand speed of 150 words per minute. What you will need, if you are to make the grade, is an ability to type and take shorthand both quickly and accurately, and a sound knowledge of English. You will have to understand fully what is being said, even if the matters are technical or the evidence is given ungrammatically, so that you can take clear notes and produce a transcript which is grammatically correct, easily understandable and retains the original sense of what was said.

### Training
The training of court reporters is undertaken by firms in London and the provinces which have appointments from the Lord Chancellor to record court proceedings. The addresses of those companies can be obtained from either the Institute of Shorthand Writers, or the Association of Professional Shorthand Writers (see pp 122 and 123).

The length of training rather depends upon the skill you have when you start. If you have good speeds and experience in either law or the business world, you may well be able to complete your training in anything from three months to a year; without that experience it will take longer. Methods of training differ from firm to firm. Usually, a trainee is seconded to work with a more experienced court reporter who will help with specialised techniques and will be able to give the trainee advice on editing and preparing the transcripts. By working in the courts you will improve your speeds and develop an understanding of legal procedure and terminology.

The Lord Chancellor's Department is committed to the use of computer-aided transcription in the larger court centres and new entrants to the profession will be exclusively those trained in machine shorthand.

There are about 600 court reporters nationwide of whom 70 per cent are women, though the profession is open to both sexes equally.

**Salaries**

The salaries paid to qualified court reporters are nowadays highly negotiable. Trainees are paid around £7,000 to £8,000 a year, depending which firm they are with and how much time is spent. Once trained, the basic salary is around £11,000, and will probably reach £17,000 after five years' experience. One of the advantages of the job is that the salary can reflect the amount of work that you are able and prepared to do. When you reach the stage of being able to produce daily transcripts in long cases, your earnings could well exceed £25,000pa, and even £30,000 in London.

Most court reporters work on a freelance basis, and firms often engage self-employed court reporters. The income you make is likely to be much the same, whether you are employed or self-employed.

**Scotland**

Court reporters are engaged when and where required from local firms of shorthand writers who specialise in this type of work.

**Northern Ireland**

Shorthand writers are employed in the criminal courts for the trials of more serious crimes only, and computer-aided transcription is now used extensively. Civil proceedings in the High Court are tape recorded and transcribed when notice of appeal is lodged, by members of the Supreme Court typing pool.

**Conclusion**

Court reporters have to be prepared to reach and maintain high standards in their work, and also to work irregular hours as required. Those who qualify usually find the job interesting and satisfying. You are not confined to an office, and although the same skills are always employed, no two cases are ever the same. You might spend three days recording a very technical commercial dispute, and then a week taking notes in a serious burglary case – you can never tell in advance.

# Chapter 8

# Legal Secretaries

## Introduction

As with court reporters, the majority of legal secretaries are
women. The job requires the secretary to develop specialist
knowledge of how to set out different legal documents and
how to use legal terminology, as well as the usual secretarial
skills. Some secretaries are employed in barristers' chambers or
by Faculty Services Limited (see p 123) or by other professionals
mentioned in this book; some are employed in courts and in
government departments. However, most legal secretaries work
in solicitors' offices. In all these jobs they have to master particular
formats and procedures.

## Training

You might have the opportunity of taking typing and shorthand
lessons at school, but while these skills are helpful they are by no
means essential. What is important for school-leavers who want to
become legal secretaries, is that they should have a good grasp of
English and that they should have learned how to spell. It should be
stressed that many legal secretaries have a high academic standard,
and agencies are often concerned to know how many GCSE passes
prospective secretaries have. At least as important as this are an
ability to work under pressure, common sense, and a willingness
to use initiative and take responsibility.

Legal secretaries, like any others, need to have good typing
speeds. For an audio secretary, speeds of around 55 words per
minute are usually required. Shorthand dictation is much less
common now than in the past.

Some secretaries start in an office and learn as they go; others
take courses at their local colleges of further education or private
schools. However, in 1976 the Association of Legal Secretaries was

established in England and Wales and the Association has devised recognised and validated courses leading to qualifications of the Association. A number of colleges run courses leading to the Legal Secretary's Certificate and the Legal Secretary's Diploma. A list of the centres offering courses leading to these two qualifications can be obtained direct from the Association of Legal Secretaries (see p 122).

In addition, various courses are available at colleges of further education which, though not specifically aimed at legal secretaries, are designed to teach the basic skills all secretaries in commerce will require. Courses can take account of the different academic qualifications that students may have, and different courses lead to different qualifications – many result in the Royal Society of Arts Diploma; others result in local Chamber of Commerce awards. In some instances, private schools have their own diplomas.

## How to Find a Job

Whether you have a qualification or are looking for a job straight from school, one of the best ways of finding a vacancy is to keep an eye out for advertisements in newspapers. Local and evening papers often have ads for legal secretaries, and you will soon find which paper in your area is the best bet. *The Times*, the *Scotsman* and the *Belfast Telegraph* all carry ads for the higher grade PA secretarial jobs, and it is certainly worth looking there if this is the type of work you are after. There may be vacancies in Jobcentres and there are also private employment agencies, some of which specialise in legal secretarial jobs. As with other jobs in the law, you should never forget to ask around when looking for a post. If you have contacts and friends in solicitors' offices they may well hear of vacancies that are never otherwise advertised.

### The Interview

The important thing to establish at an interview is what the firm actually wants from you. When 'senior secretary' is stated, does this mean an audio typist who has to work for three fee-earners? Is a 'copy typist' a general office clerk? Make sure the role suits you. Do not ask general questions such as 'Will I be able to take on more responsibility?' – the answer to that will not tell you very much. Ask specific questions, such as 'Will I get to meet the clients?', 'What else will I be expected to do, other than type?', 'How many people will I actually work for?'.

When you go for an interview you will probably know what pay is being offered, but don't forget to ask about any system the firm has for reviewing salaries or upgrading staff. Ask if it is possible to be promoted within the organisation (it is not so in all firms, as some regard the practice of offering a higher grade job to someone who is already employed at a lower grade as divisive). Check when you can take your first holiday – most firms specify that employees have to work some months before they earn any holiday entitlement so you might have to wait longer than you were expecting. See if additional days' leave are awarded with length of service, and how long you can take off at one time. Find out who you will be answerable to – it might not always be the person you work for if he or she is junior in the organisation. It may be possible at the time of the interview to meet the person you would be working for, or to see the office you would be working in – never be afraid to ask. The interview will not answer all your questions but the more you find out at that stage the better chance you will have of making the right choice.

## The Work

Legal secretaries, like solicitors, tend to specialise in particular areas of the law. You will probably find that you will gain experience in one field (say, conveyancing) and then be even more valuable in the eyes of a prospective employer, who will know that you can be left not only to type what is dictated accurately and in the correct format, but also to recognise the right forms to use and to fill them in with a minimum of explanation. You will know when to take copies, when to provide enclosures and what to tell clients who ring up to find out how their cases are progressing. Some firms allow experienced secretaries in conveyancing departments to attend completions, or experienced secretaries in litigation departments to attend court to take notes of the proceedings. Indeed, some legal secretaries become sufficiently interested in the law that they go on to qualify as legal executives or even solicitors.

Many people considering legal secretarial work think that they will be personal assistants to their bosses, but there are relatively few openings of this kind. One of the reasons for this is that solicitors tend to use trainee solicitors to do some of their administrative chores, since their training consists of learning office practice as well as law. In addition, the almost universal use of audio machines means that secretaries spend little time taking dictation from their bosses and are therefore less likely to become involved in the cases, beyond typing the correspondence and documents. Further, legal secretaries are, of course, at a premium and if you have any time left over after typing for one person, a firm will often consider that the most economical use of your time is for you to type for someone else as well. Very often legal secretaries find that they are kept busy typing and developing other technical skills, such as operating wordprocessing and telex machines, rather than becoming directly involved in the cases and having very much contact with clients. However, there are legal personal assistant jobs around and if that is what you have in mind, follow up the advertisements that ask specifically for PAs.

**Temporary Work**
Some legal secretaries prefer to do temporary work. Temps are employed by agencies who hire out their services to firms who become short-staffed or over-worked for a while. The firms pay the agencies on an hourly rate and the agencies pay the secretaries. Usually, temporary work pays better than a permanent job, but the real benefit is that you get as much flexibility as you can afford. You are paid for the hours you work, and if you want a day off you just inform the agency in advance. Of course, when there is less work about you run the risk of not being able to work as long as you might wish to, but many people prefer to run that risk in order to be able to organise their days to suit themselves, or to fit in with family commitments. It can also be exciting to go to different offices – you get changes of scene and meet many more people. You also get wide-ranging experience in office procedures (which differ from firm to firm) and real self-confidence from knowing you are good enough at your job to be able to just walk in and pick up the threads.

**Salary**

The salary you could earn as a legal secretary will depend on the size of the firm you join, the grade of job you get, the amount of experience you have and the part of the country in which you work.

Most firms make a distinction between office juniors (who do mainly copy typing for anyone in the firm who needs help), secretaries (who work for legal executives, articled clerks, and assistant solicitors), and partners' secretaries. The current rates of pay for partners' secretaries in London range from £10,000 upwards. Outside the larger cities, rates tend to be lower – junior typists in the provinces in England and Wales can expect to start at around £5,500, with partners' secretaries earning from about £8,000 upwards.

In Scotland, the higher wages are paid in Edinburgh and Aberdeen, followed by Glasgow and Dundee, and again, jobs in rural areas are less well paid.

In Northern Ireland, the salary structure is not as formalised as in the rest of the UK and salaries can vary from £5,000 upwards.

For the wage rates in your area, check with your local Jobcentre or private agencies.

## Conclusion

For legal secretaries, standards are rising and you will have to be prepared to offer more in terms of ability than most office workers. You will be given responsibility and be expected to shoulder it; you will have to get used to being accurate and checking everything you do, and you will have to be able to work under pressure. If you are meeting clients, you will have to be smart and well groomed.

In return, you will receive higher than average wages for a secretary and, as you have a specialist skill, you will be more likely to have job security. You should find it easier to change jobs if you want to, and your skills will be welcome anywhere in the UK, although you would have to be prepared to adjust to the differences in legal procedures between the three jurisdictions. Even more important is the fact that most legal secretaries find their jobs worthwhile. It is nice to know that by doing your job well you are also helping others to do theirs, and certainly most solicitors would agree that good legal secretaries are worth a great deal. Knowing that you are appreciated is a large perk in any job!

*Case Study*
Trisha

When I left school I had a couple of jobs before I thought of becoming a secretary. I didn't have any O levels or secretarial training, and in fact the first job I had in a solicitor's office was in the accounts department – I hated it! Then at the end of my first month the office manageress told me they had a vacancy for a junior on the switchboard, so I took it.

The office, which was in North Wales, was quite small and so, when I wasn't too busy on the switchboard, I was encouraged to do some typing to help out. I started off copy typing wills and leases that weren't urgently required, and that way I came to see how basic legal documents are set out. My typing speeds improved and I became more accurate. When the junior typist in the general office left, I was offered her job. In the general office I learned more about the usual office procedures – I sorted post, acted as a receptionist, ran errands, took messages, filed documents, kept records, and made tea – and I was still improving my typing skills.

After a couple of years I came to London. I had enough experience by then to get a job as a secretary to an assistant solicitor, and then I became a partner's secretary. When I was working in the office in Wales I got rather impatient sometimes – I used to feel I always got the most mundane tasks and that I could take on more responsibility than I was given, but looking back I realise I had an excellent training. Knowing how an office runs means I do my job better – I know not only what to do but why it is necessary and how to organise my work accordingly.

Like most legal secretaries I have specialised, and although I have worked in litigation and matrimonial departments, most of my experience has been in probate and conveyancing. As a result I know the procedure and can explain to clients what stage has been reached, and what remains to be done. I've also witnessed wills and have been sent to carry out completions on house purchases, all of which adds to the interest of the job.

# Chapter 9

# Law Costs Draftsmen

## Introduction

The work of a solicitor has to be paid for, and, although solicitors often process their own bills there are many instances when they turn to law costs draftsmen to prepare formal bills for them.

Most solicitors operate a system of time recording, and bill their clients according to how long a case has taken and whether the work was done by a senior or junior member of staff. Increasingly, the recording of the time spent by solicitors is computerised, along with their accounting systems. Apart from the amount of time spent on a case, a great number of rules and regulations surround the level of costs solicitors can charge. Some bills are paid by clients direct; others are paid by another party, or out of public funds if the client is entitled to legal aid. Therefore, the procedure of drawing bills can be technical and time-consuming, and so the specialised job of the law costs draftsman (usually known as costs draftsman) has developed.

There are no qualifications required for entry into this profession, though you will need to have a facility with figures and, in common with virtually all careers in the law, a good standard of English, both written and spoken, is necessary.

To be able to cope with the work, you will probably need to have academic standards at least equivalent to trainee legal executives (see p 72). Equally as important as academic qualifications will be the personal qualities you can bring to the job. You will need patience and an ability to cope with detail, and if you are preparing accounts – particularly from other people's records – you need to be methodical and careful.

## Training

No particular training is required for law costs draftsmen, who, despite the name, may be women or men. In the past, many came to the job either from an accounts department or as legal executives who found they had gained experience and interest in this specialised work.

However, in 1977 the Association of Law Costs Draftsmen (see p 122) was formed. The Association operates in England and Northern Ireland, and membership is open to men and women over the age of 18 years who are employed as law costs draftsmen. The Association publishes a newsletter to keep members abreast of changes in practice and the rules of taxation. The Association aims to promote the status of the profession and the maintenance of standards, and has established a network of counsellors to whom prospective students can apply for initial advice on taking up a career as law costs draftsmen. If you wish to contact a counsellor you should write to the secretary of the Association.

As yet there is no independent organisation of law costs draftsmen in Scotland, but good training can be obtained from working in a solicitors' office where you will pick up the basic rules behind solicitors' billing. Increasingly, law costs draftsmen are setting up independent companies, and you might find a company prepared to take you on from school and train you, if you show sufficient aptitude and interest.

## The Work

Whether employed by a firm of solicitors or working independently, a law costs draftsman will be given all the solicitor's files and papers relating to a case and asked to draw up a bill. The first task is often to sort out the file, to see what correspondence there has been, what action the solicitor has taken on behalf of the client, who has done the work – whether it was a partner or an assistant solicitor, a managing clerk, or a trainee – and how long it took. The law costs draftsman also sees what expenses have been incurred; the solicitor may well have had to pay travelling expenses or court fees, and a barrister/advocate may have been engaged on the case.

Having established what work has been done, the law costs draftsman has to see what scale of charges is allowable in the particular instances of a case. For instance, if the bill is to be paid by the losing party in a civil action, the person concerned can only be asked to pay the costs directly related to the action. So, if the solicitor has spent more time on a case because, for instance, the client rang up every day to enquire about the progress, that part of the solicitor's bill has to be isolated and charged to the client.

Sometimes a solicitor's account may be challenged by a client, and solicitors are not always able to show how the costing was arrived at in relation to the regulations. In these circumstances the account will be referred to law costs draftsmen. As a highly experienced law costs draftswoman remarked:

> Please do not think these bills are unreasonable. They probably are not, but I am aware that a great many of them are not based on the formal method of charging which would be employed if the rules were to be strictly observed. In many cases, solicitors who are inexperienced under-charge rather than over-charge.

Courts have various powers to vet solicitors' bills, and when this happens, bills are said to be subject to 'taxation'. Since the law costs draftsman knows precisely which scales apply in what instances, and what can and cannot be charged in different cases, he or she is regularly asked to attend taxations (which are conducted before taxing masters in the High Court and registrars in the county courts), either to defend the bills they themselves have drawn up, or to oppose the bills drawn up by others. The court then decides what fees and expenses are properly allowable, and good law costs draftsmen, who know the rules and procedures, can save solicitors and their clients considerable amounts of money. In this way they usually spend one day a week in court, and the rest of the time in the office sorting paperwork and drafting bills.

While some law costs draftsmen are employed in solicitors' offices, increasingly they are employed by independent law costs draftsmen's firms, or work as self-employed individuals for such firms, or on their own. Not all work in an office: many collect files from solicitors' offices or from the company office, and work at home. This can be very advantageous to married people, who can continue to develop their careers while fitting their work in with the demands of home and family.

## Prospects

If arithmetic does not scare you, and you enjoy being a bit of a detective, this work might well appeal to you. The profession is not large (the Association has only 250 members at present) but it appears to be growing, and for self-employed law costs draftsmen the rates of pay are very competitive compared with other office jobs for which no formal qualifications are needed.

There is no defined career structure. You will earn more as your experience grows and you handle larger cases. There is certainly plenty of work available at the moment and that condition will probably carry on for as long as the system of legal costing continues.

Law costs draftsmen provide a service for solicitors and their clients which is both necessary and appreciated, and the work can be rewarding both financially and in terms of job satisfaction.

## Salary

If you are employed in a solicitor's office, you will probably earn roughly the same as a legal executive. If you work for a firm or are self-employed, you are usually paid a percentage of the profit costs (ie solicitors' fees) calculated in a bill. Hard work is often well rewarded.

*Chapter 10*
# Court Workers

## Introduction

The smooth running of the day-to-day business of the courts throughout the UK is maintained by court administrators and clerical staff. There are many different jobs at various grades, some of which you can enter straight from school and others which require previous training, but they are all responsible jobs in which you will be encouraged to use your initiative.

Jobs in the courts are open to men and women, and to both school-leavers and more mature applicants alike. A career with the court service is secure, and what attracts most people are the possibilities for career development rather than financial incentives. Promotion is generally made from lower grades, which allows beginners to move up through the service as they gain experience, and training is often made available.

## Magistrates' Courts

Each magistrates' court is organised by a local magistrates' courts' committee, although initial enquiries about careers in magistrates' courts should be referred to C2 Division of the Home Office (see also p 65).

Clerical and administrative work is undertaken in magistrates' courts by justices' clerks' assistants. They are not civil servants, but nonetheless enjoy a secure living and pension rights similar to their colleagues in other courts.

To work in a magistrates' court you may need O level English or its equivalent, but many applicants, in fact, have A levels or degrees. Training in office and administrative procedure and elementary law is given to beginners, and there are courses provided as you gain experience.

In the Justices' Clerks' Departments the minimum wage for a

clerical officer aged 16 years is £4,776 at the time of writing. For those over the age of 21 years the scale runs up to £6,837. Administrative grades earn between £7,518 and £13,473 (latest available figures).

**The Lord Chancellor's Department**
The Lord Chancellor's Department is a major government department with wide responsibilities for the administration of justice in England and Wales. Since 1972 it has been responsible for the day-to-day administration of all the higher courts (ie County and Crown Courts, the High Court and Court of Appeal – magistrates' courts are administered by the Home Office) and it is in carrying out this function that most of the Department's 11,000 or so staff are employed.

The running of the 400 or more courts that fall within the Department's responsibility could clearly not all be handled from London, where the Department has its headquarters, and so for this purpose the country (ie England and Wales – the Scottish Court Service is administered by the Scottish Courts Administration and the courts in Northern Ireland by the Northern Ireland Court Service) is divided into six regional areas which are known as 'Circuits'. Each Circuit is headed by a senior official – the 'Circuit Administrator' – who is responsible for the smooth running of the groups of courts within his area. Approximately 8,000 of the Department's staff work in the regions and are directly involved in the day-to-day business of the courts; the remainder work in London.

**Jobs in the courts**
The Lord Chancellor's Department can offer a varied and interesting career connected with the law. Entry is usually at one of three main levels: Administrative Assistant; Administrative Officer or Executive Officer. The type of work will depend substantially upon the grade at which staff are employed. The following gives an indication of what can be expected:

*Administrative Assistant*
This is the first rung of the administrative staff ladder. The duties tend to be routine and typically involve keeping records, sorting and filing papers, and some simple figure-work, perhaps using a calculator. There may be some straightforward letter-writing and time spent dealing with enquiries from the public. The job is very much like that of a junior clerk in a large business firm, with

neatness and accuracy as the prime virtues. There is no typing – that is a separate job – but Administrative Assistants in some offices may be employed on other kinds of keyboard operation. The grade has no supervisory role and is supervised by Executive Officers and higher grades.

*Administrative Officer*

This is the main clerical grade in the Civil Service. The duties call for the exercise of discretion and initiative within set guidelines. Administrative Officers handle incoming correspondence; they write or draft letters; they give all kinds of advice and assistance to the public, either over the telephone or across the counter; they assess fees and payments, and they check accounts and keep statistics and various records. They sometimes work with Administrative Assistants but they are given – and are expected to accept – more responsibility. Many Administrative Officer posts in the Lord Chancellor's Department are in areas which are subject to heavy workload pressures, such as in the 300 or so County Courts where speed and reliability are among the essential qualities.

*Executive Officer*

The Executive Officer grade is the first level in the administration group of Civil Service grades in which the management and supervision of staff are likely to constitute a significant part of the work. In a County Court, an Executive Officer could expect to head a small team of Administrative Assistants/Officers and would be responsible for organising them and their work. He or she would also deal with complex or difficult situations which the administrative staff could not be expected to handle, for example the problems posed by particularly angry or distressed members of the public. By contrast, a new Executive Officer in a Crown Court would not normally have a staff management responsibility but would start work as a Court Clerk, sitting in court with the Judge and swearing-in the jury, taking the defendant's plea, keeping a brief note of the proceedings and assessing the fees claimed by the barristers. After about a year as a Court Clerk, he or she might then move on to another area of Crown Court work (for example, the listing of court cases) which might involve an element of staff supervision.

About 50 per cent of Executive Officer posts are in the County Courts and 10 per cent in the Crown Courts, but there are also opportunities outside these areas, for example in the Department's headquarters in London (personnel, finance, accommodation, training etc), in the High Court in the Royal Courts of Justice, or in a number of associated offices and tribunals.

**Qualifications**
The following are the normal minimum requirements for the grades:

*Administrative Assistant*: Two acceptable (Grade C or above) passes at GCSE, of which one must be in English language.

*Administrative Officer*: Five acceptable passes (Grade C or above) at GCSE, of which one must be in English language.

Administrative Assistants and Administrative Officers are recruited locally (in all areas except London), so contact your local careers office, Jobcentre or the Chief Clerk of your local County or Crown Court for details of the vacancies available. Recruitment in the London area is carried out by a Central Recruitment Unit, which can be contacted at the Lord Chancellor's Department, 81 Chancery Lane, London WC2., It may be possible for applicants without formal educational qualifications to sit a written test to determine whether they might be suitable for interview.

*Executive Officer*: Recruitment to the Executive Officer grade is dealt with by the Civil Service Commission at Alencon Link (see p 122). You will be asked by the Commission to state your preference for departments, and you should at this stage identify the Lord Chancellor's Department as your preferred posting.

You may contact the Lord Chancellor's Department direct for further details of career opportunities in the courts (see p 124) and it is worth noting that vacancies in the Department are often advertised in the press.

**Scotland**

The Scottish Courts Administration is responsible for employing the administrative and clerical staff for the Scottish Court Service. A clerk grade equates to a clerical officer in the Civil Service (salary scale £3,306–£6,671). The salary scale for Second Class Deputes (EO equivalent) is £5,250–£9,452 (latest figures available, March 1989).

## Northern Ireland

Court staff are members of the NI Court Service which is part of the Lord Chancellor's Department. The headquarters of the Court Service is located at Windsor House, 9–15 Bedford Street, Belfast BT2 7LT. Entry into the administrative grade is at two levels, Administrative Officer and Administrative Assistant. An Administrative Officer's salary commences at £3,873 (age 16) and runs to £6,386 for those aged 20. The maximum of the scale stands at £7,555. An Administrative Assistant's pay commences at £67.49 per week (age 16) and rises to a maximum of £116.49 (latest figures available).

*Chapter 11*
# Other Jobs in the Law

## Introduction

Apart from the careers already mentioned, you might find an opening in one of the jobs which are either closely allied to, or service the legal profession as a whole. This chapter is intended to give a brief résumé of a few of these alternatives.

## Patent Agents

There are currently some 1,250 patent agents on the UK Register of Patent Agents and, while there is no requirement for them to have formal legal qualifications, their work involves a considerable knowledge of the law of patents, copyright and trademarks, both here and abroad.

The government runs the Patent Office as part of the Department of Trade and Industry. This deals with about 40,000 applications per year from inventors who want a patent granted for their invention. The grant of patent means that an inventor can stop people using his or her invention without permission for 20 years. The growing complexity of the system of registration, added to the fact that inventors are now more commonly companies than private individuals, has led to the growth of a small profession of people whose primary function is to act on behalf of inventors in registering their inventions both with the UK Patent Office and abroad.

The work of a patent agent involves drafting and revising patent specifications and licence agreements. A patent agent will often be asked to advise on the validity of patents or on whether a patent or trademark is being infringed. It is not at all uncommon for patent agents to bring proceedings on behalf of clients where there has been an infringement, and some will even appear for clients in the Patent Court, on appeals from decisions of the Patent Office, rather than engage barristers to do so.

To be a patent agent requires a rather unusual blend of skills: legal, linguistic and technical. Most patent agents have a degree in a science subject and receive in-house training at work. For those who make the grade it can be both interesting and financially rewarding. Further details can be obtained from the Chartered Institute of Patent Agents (see p 122).

## Teachers

Some lawyers prefer to teach rather than practise in the mainstream of the legal profession. The level of academic qualifications required varies depending on the level at which you wish to teach. University lecturers usually have a first class or upper second class LLB or BA, and the majority will also have a Masters degree and a professional qualification. However, law is also taught in polytechnics and colleges of further education, both separately and as part of other courses, and in these cases the academic requirements for teachers may not be so high. Professional colleges, such as the College of Law and the Inns of Court School of Law in England and Wales and the Institute of Professional Legal Studies in Northern Ireland, also employ teachers. In these there will be greater emphasis on the teachers' understanding of the requirements of the profession which the student is to enter.

The universities and polytechnics advertise their vacancies in the national press, and details of vacancies can be obtained from the colleges or departments direct. In the case of colleges of further education, information can be obtained from the Local Education Authority in the area in which the college is situated. Some colleges advertise posts in professional magazines, such as *The Law Society's Gazette* and the *Journal of the Law Society of Scotland* (see p 119).

If you want to teach, you will need more than a good degree. You must have a genuine interest in the subject area you are going to teach, as well as a wish to communicate your enthusiasm to others. Certainly at higher levels of education you will need an interest in ideas for their own sake, as well as an ability to lecture and write.

Many people think of teaching as an easy option which gives secure employment and long holidays. However, teaching has its own problems (such as keeping up to date with the subject material) and you should make sure before you set out that you know the genuine advantages and disadvantages.

The pressures of teaching are usually less than those experienced by barristers/advocates and solicitors but they do exist. Many teachers have to be prepared to teach for five hours a day and, like any stand-up comic, they can die on their audience! Also, the jobs, while relatively secure and pensioned, usually pay only two-thirds as much as is earned by solicitors or barristers/advocates with comparable experience. Like all jobs, teaching has its boring moments, and most teachers dread the annual round of setting examinations and marking papers.

Teachers probably have greater control than barristers/advocates or solicitors over the way they spend their days, and they also have the advantage that their skills can more readily be transferred to other countries outside the UK.

## Company Secretaries and Chartered Secretaries

The role of a company secretary is one recognised in legislation, which requires that company secretaries of public limited companies be professionally qualified. This places the company secretary in a unique position *vis-à-vis* the board of directors.

The company secretary is the officer who is ostensibly the company's chief administrator. However, a company secretary's actual function will vary from company to company.

Company secretaries, whether of public or private companies, deal with aspects of management which relate to the company as a legal entity. They keep the company records; make the company's tax returns; advise the board of directors of their legal obligations and arrange company meetings, collecting information for them and recording the decisions. In many companies, the company secretary will have a direct legal or financial function and will possibly also be involved in personnel management. Company secretaries are administrators who assist in management, planning and the general running of the company.

As the responsibilities and needs of the job have grown, the role has been established on a more professional basis. Many company secretaries in private companies have legal qualifications and many others, particularly in larger organisations, are members of the Institute of Chartered Secretaries and Administrators, which holds exams in June and December of each year leading to the qualification of Chartered Secretary.

Opportunities for chartered secretaries are considerable, as the skills they have are required by many organisations and there is plenty of scope for specialisation and moving into general management and administration at the highest level. As already mentioned, some become company secretaries, but others work in industry, commerce, city financial institutions, the public services, and the law, where large firms of solicitors often employ partnership secretaries (see p 108). Full details of the training and qualification of chartered secretaries are available from the Institute (see p 123).


## Notaries

Notaries are public officers who are appointed to draw up, authenticate and certify deeds and documents, such as conveyances and powers of attorney concerning property both here and abroad. They are also called upon to certify transactions relating to negotiable instruments (for example bills of exchange) which are used when there is a foreign element to the transaction. They are appointed by the Court of Faculties of the Archbishop of Canterbury, but with the exception of ecclesiastical notaries, they are not concerned with church matters.

A notary's certificate on any document is important, since it is recognised anywhere in the world. Notaries are often called upon to witness signatures on legal documents, and they are also able to prepare wills and other important legal papers.

There are three types of notary: ecclesiastical notaries who are usually diocesan registrars or legal secretaries to bishops; scrivener notaries; and general notaries.

Scrivener notaries constitute a very small, separate profession practising in central London. No other notaries are authorised to practise in that area. They have their own training system, which involves serving an apprenticeship of five years with a practising notary, and taking exams in English legal subjects, foreign languages and foreign law. One year of their apprenticeship is served abroad. Apprentices do not study criminal law or legal procedure, however, since notaries do not have a right of audience before the courts as solicitors do. Instead, they take additional exams in subjects such as private international law; the law of ships and shipping; bills of exchange; two foreign languages and notarial practice. The exams are under the direction of the Scriveners' Company – a City livery company – and, if you wish to practise in central London within the area of the Company, you have to obtain a certificate from the Company before you can apply to the Court of Faculties of the Archbishop of Canterbury for a certificate to practise as a notary. The standard required for those wishing to train as scrivener notaries is high, and the openings are few.

Enquiries should be addressed to the Society of Public Notaries of London (see p 124).

General notaries – who are normally also solicitors – have to serve an apprenticeship of five years and can practise in all parts of England and Wales outside central London. Prior to admission they have to sit various examinations set by the Court of Faculties.

In Scotland if you wish to be a public notary you must first be enrolled as a solicitor and then petition the Inner House of the Court of Session. About half of all practising newly qualified Scots solicitors become notaries and full details of the requirements for becoming a notary in Scotland can be obtained from the Clerk to the Administration of Notaries, WHS Balfour, 58 Frederick Street, Edinburgh.

## Other Jobs in Solicitors' Offices

### Partnership Secretaries
Increasingly, large firms of solicitors are finding that they need the administrative skills of a partnership secretary. Like company secretaries in industry, the functions of partnership secretaries differ in different organisations, but they are usually individuals with either company secretarial or accountancy qualifications. An ability to manage computerised accounting systems will be an asset. Partnership secretaries have high-status jobs which pay high salaries.

In small firms the functions of a partnership secretary are usually undertaken by one of the partners, assisted by the firm's accountant.

### General Office Staff
Most firms of solicitors have a general office with staff consisting of messengers and clerks, whose job it is to collect and deliver papers, distribute incoming post, and collect up and frank outgoing mail. Sometimes the 'general office' is in charge of the firm's photocopying, and sometimes these staff act as receptionists as well. As a school-leaver, you could start in a general office without any very clear idea of what you want to do, or what alternatives are available to you, but having found your feet you might wish to move into other areas.

### Outdoor Clerks
In England and Wales and Northern Ireland, when solicitors tell clients they have issued a writ or taken out a summons, what they

usually mean is that they have filled out the correct forms and handed them to the outdoor clerk who goes to the court and ensures that any necessary fees are paid and that the documents are stamped by the court. The outdoor clerk also lodges papers in court before hearings and obtains dates for court appointments. Sometimes applications for a hearing are simply put on a list and allocated a date by the court later, and in those cases it is up to the outdoor clerk to keep a check on the court lists and notify the solicitor when a hearing date is given. As an outdoor clerk becomes more experienced, he or she may also be asked to attend court on simple procedural applications. As an outdoor clerk, you would be out of the office most days of the week and would quickly learn both office and court procedure.

Outdoor clerks are often given their own files to work on. Very often they start off with debt collection matters, in which their knowledge of court procedure, and particularly of how judgments are enforced, is very useful. Some end up as managing clerks or go on to qualify as legal executives or solicitors, but others prefer to remain as outdoor clerks throughout their careers.

There are no particular academic qualifications required, although you will need to be physically fit, have a good standard of spoken English, and be able to communicate well. Small firms may not employ an outdoor clerk and instead may ask a messenger to do the necessary work. However, most large firms which take on litigation work will produce enough court work to need an outdoor clerk. Salaries start from about £6,000 pa.

In Scotland most large firms employ messengers, but seldom employ outdoor clerks as those in England, Wales and Northern Ireland do.

**Clerical Work**
All firms have staff dealing with their accounting, and the size of the department will depend on the size of the firm. Some firms employ only one qualified accountant, while others have enough work to warrant taking on half-a-dozen school-leavers, as well as a number of qualified staff. Many firms now have computerised accounting systems, and you would have to be prepared to learn how to operate them, if necessary. Ilex Tutorial Services has recently introduced a legal accountancy course and exams in legal accountancy are held by the Institute of Legal Executives twice a year. Full details are available from the Institute (see p 123).

# Part 2

# Chapter 12

# Courses

## Degree Courses in Law

Degree courses are provided by universities, polytechnics and colleges of further education. They are usually full-time three-year courses, but some part-time courses, usually four or five years in length, are provided. Degree courses may lead to your being awarded a Bachelor of Law (LLB) or a Bachelor of Arts (BA). The BA courses are usually more broadly based, and are often awarded when law has been combined with some other subject. Combined courses are becoming more widely available, and on these courses law is often taught with social or political sciences.

The course content for each degree course differs widely between institutions. Always look at the syllabus of any course you propose to take to ensure that the topics covered are those you want to study. A prospectus can be obtained from the Faculty or Department of Law at the university, polytechnic or college.

To know what qualifications you will need before you stand a chance of getting a place on a degree course, check with the institution to which you are applying and make sure that the course you are to follow will enable you to obtain an exemption from taking the basic academic requirements of the profession you wish to enter, if you intend to go straight into professional training once you have been awarded a degree. Most courses will enable you to claim an exemption but not all. Combined courses in particular may not cover all the core subjects, so check with the institution. Do remember that a degree received from a university in England and Wales is unlikely to provide an exemption from the Scottish or Northern Irish professional exams. Equally, degrees obtained from Scotland or Northern Ireland are unlikely to provide an exemption in the other jurisdictions. Only Dundee in Scotland provides its law graduates with the necessary subject passes to entitle them to full exemption from the CPE in England and Wales. It is therefore a good idea, when choosing a university, to consider carefully where in the UK you intend to practise in the future.

Many people applying for a place on a first degree course are entitled to a grant from their local authority. Entitlement to a grant is linked to your parents' income, if you have been living at home just prior to starting your course. Ask for details from your local education authority or from your town hall.

Most people go on to degree courses immediately on leaving school. To be able to start a course in the autumn term in the same year as you take your A levels, you will need to have applied in the December of the year before you take your A levels. Places will usually be offered which are conditional upon your attaining the necessary A level grades.

You can make applications to five universities through the Universities' Central Council on Admissions (UCCA) which circulates details of your academic record to the universities, who will either offer you a place on the strength of your past achievements or ask you along for an interview. UCCA forms are usually provided by schools, but you can get in touch with UCCA by writing to them at PO Box 28, Cheltenham, Gloucestershire; tel 0242 222444. Applications can also be made direct to the institutions of your choice, but this approach is more likely to succeed if you already have your A level results.

Those wishing to apply to Oxford or Cambridge are required to take a special entrance paper, and places are offered on the basis of the results achieved in this rather than in A level examinations. The entrance exams are held in the autumn term of each year and you should ask your school for details.

In Scotland, at the time of writing, only five universities offer first degree courses in law, namely Aberdeen, Dundee, Edinburgh, Glasgow and Strathclyde. In Northern Ireland, only Queen's University in Belfast offers a course leading to an LLB. However, there are many institutions offering such courses in England and Wales, and in deciding which courses to apply for you may find the following publications helpful:

*A Degree Course Guide – Law* by R J Smith. Published by Hobsons Press (Cambridge) Limited, Bateman Street, Cambridge CB2 1LZ.

*University Entrance: The Official Guide*. Published annually by the Committee of Vice-Chancellors and Principals of the United Kingdom Universities, 29 Tavistock Square, London WC1.

*Directory of First Degree and Diploma of Higher Education Courses;
Directory of Postgraduate and Post-Experience Courses.* Published
by the Council for National Academic Awards, 344–354 Gray's
Inn Road, London WC1X 8BP, available from them free, or from
polytechnics.

*British Qualifications.* An annual publication. Published by Kogan Page
Limited, 120 Pentonville Road, London N1 9JN.

## Professional Training Courses

### England and Wales

*Solicitors*
Recognised courses leading to the SFE are held at various centres
and, although at the time of writing it was not known which
institutions would offer the Legal Practice Course when it comes
into effect, the LPC is likely to be offered by a broad range of
institutions throughout the country. Details can be obtained from
the Law Society, which regularly produces booklets about entry
into the profession and the opportunities available within it.

*Barristers*
Courses leading to the Diploma in Law are run by:

City University, Legal Studies Unit, Northampton Square, London EC1V
0HB
Polytechnic of Central London, The School Officer for Law, Red Lion
Square, London WC1R 4SR

Courses leading to the Bar Examination are run by:

The Inns of Court, School of Law, 4 Gray's Inn Place, London WC1R
5DX

### Scotland

*Solicitors*
There are no courses leading to the Law Society of Scotland's
professional examinations.

Courses leading to the Diploma in Legal Practice are run by the
five universities offering first degree courses in law in Scotland and

details can be obtained direct from the universities, namely:

Aberdeen University, University Office, Regent Walk, Aberdeen AB9
  1FX; 0224 272000
Dundee University, Park Road, Dundee DD1 4HN; 0382 23181
Edinburgh University, Old College, South Bridge, Edinburgh EH8 9YL;
  031–650 1000
Glasgow University, University Avenue, Glasgow G12 8QQ; 041–339
  8855
Strathclyde University, The Law School, Stenhouse Building, 173
  Cathedral Street, Glasgow G4 0RQ; 041–552 4400

*Advocates*
Courses leading to the Faculty Examinations are also run by the
five universities listed above.

## Northern Ireland

*Solicitors*
Courses leading to the Certificate of Professional Legal Studies
are held at the Institute of Professional Legal Studies at Queen's
University, Belfast BT7 1NN and enquiries should be sent to the
Director of the Institute.

*Barristers*
Barristers are also required to obtain the Certificate of Professional
Legal Studies having taken a course at the Institute (see above).

## Civil Service
In England and Wales and Scotland, once you have obtained a job
in one of the Civil Service departments, you will be sent on training
courses arranged by your employing department or at the Civil
Service College. Information on these courses may be obtained
from the employing departments.
   Full details of training for the Civil Service of Northern Ireland
can be obtained from the Civil Service Commission, Rosepark
House, Upper Newtownards Road, Belfast BT4 3NR.

## Justices' Clerks
Information on courses and training available for justices' clerks
may be obtained from C2 Division, Home Office, 50 Queen Anne's
Gate, London SW1H 9AT.

## Legal Executives

There are full-time, part-time and evening courses leading to the part one and part two examinations held at some 120 polytechnics and colleges throughout England and Wales. A list of all these institutions can be obtained from the Institute of Legal Executives, Kempston Manor, Kempston, Bedford MK42 7AB. Correspondence courses are available from Ilex Tutorial Services at Kempston Manor, Kempston, Bedford MK42 7AB.

## Barristers' Clerks

Full details of courses and training for barristers' clerks in England and Wales can be obtained from the Institute of Barristers' Clerks, Ground Floor, 2 Garden Court, Temple, London EC4Y 7EB.

## Court Reporters

Full details of courses and training for court reporters in England and Wales can be obtained from the Careers Officer, Institute of Shorthand Writers, 2 New Square, Lincoln's Inn, London WC2A 3RU, and also from the Secretary, Association of Professional Shorthand Writers, G Leigh, 6 Jelleyman Close, Blakebrook, Kidderminster DY11 6AI.

## Legal Secretaries

There are a number of colleges providing full-time courses to the Legal Secretary's Certificate and the Legal Secretary's Diploma. Full details can be obtained from the Association of Legal Secretaries, The Mill, Clymping Street, Clymping, Nr Littlehampton, Sussex BN17 5RN.

## Court Workers

For details of career opportunities in the courts, contact the Lord Chancellor's Department, Personnel Branch 3, Trevelyan House, 30 Great Peter Street, London SW1P 2BY; telephone 071–210 8682.

C2 Division, Home Office, 50 Queen Anne's Gate, London SW1H 9AT – if you are interested in justices' clerks' assistants posts.

## Patent Agents

Queen Mary College of London University, Mile End Road, London E1 4NS: two-year part-time MSc course leading to partial exemption from the Institute's exams. There is also a three-month course for a certificate in Intellectual Property Law, again leading to partial exemption.

**Company Secretaries**
There are a number of colleges providing full- and part-time courses leading to the Chartered Secretaries exams. Full details of training and the courses available can be obtained from the Institute of Chartered Secretaries and Administrators, 16 Park Crescent, London W1N 4AH.

# Chapter 13

# Useful Publications and Further Reading

## Useful Publications

All the legal professional bodies produce their own pamphlets, which are available free of charge. These give details of qualification requirements and training.

The Law Society in London keeps a list of solicitors practising in England and Wales, and this is reproduced in the *Solicitors' Diary*, which is published by Waterlow Publishers Limited. The diary lists solicitors personally and by the name and address of their firm. The Society can also supply ROSET, ie the Register of Solicitors Employing Trainees, which lists firms offering training to would-be solicitors. In Scotland a list of solicitors is printed in the *Scottish Law Directory* published by William Hodge & Co of 34–36 North Fredrick Street, Glasgow, and in Northern Ireland the Law Society of Northern Ireland publishes an annual register of solicitors.

A list of all barristers practising in England and Wales can be found in the annual *Bar List of the United Kingdom* which is published by Stevens and Sons Limited. The list gives the names of the barristers and the addresses of their chambers, and the name of the senior clerk of each chambers. There is also the *List of Barristers by Chambers*, published annually by the Holborn Law Society.

In England and Wales jobs for solicitors, legal executives, solicitors' clerks and law costs draftsmen in private practice, and vacancies in industry, government and commerce for solicitors, barristers, legal executives and solicitors' clerks are regularly advertised in: *The Times* (Tuesday's edition), the *Guardian*, the *Independent*, the *Daily Telegraph*, *The Law Society's Gazette*, the *Guardian Gazette*, the *Solicitors' Journal*, *New Law Journal*, *Local Government Chronicle*, *Legal Action Group Bulletin*, and the *Legal Executive*. In Scotland such jobs may be advertised in the *Scotsman*, the *Glasgow Herald*, the *Journal of the Law Society of Scotland*, and the *Scots Law Times*. In Northern Ireland vacancies for lawyers may be found through advertisements in the *Belfast Telegraph*, the *Belfast Newsletter*, and the *Irish News*.

## Further Reading

*Advocacy at the Bar – A Beginner's Guide* by Keith Evans (1983). Published by Financial Training Publications.

*The Art of the Advocate* by Richard Du Cann QC (new edition) (1991). Published by Pelican Books.

*Becoming a Barrister in the 80s*, a survey produced by AGCAS, available from CSU Information Booklets, Manchester.

*A Career at the Bar*, produced by The General Council of the Bar, 11 South Square, Gray's Inn, London WC1R 5EU. Free of charge.

*Careers in the Civil Service* (2nd edition) (1989). Published by Kogan Page.

*Degree Course Guide for Law*, published by CRAC, available from the Publications Office, Hobsons Ltd, Bateman Street, Cambridge CB2 1LZ.

*The Early Careers of Barristers*, a survey produced by AGCAS, available from CSU Information Booklets, Manchester.

*English Legal System* by Vanessa Stott (1981). Published by Andersen Keenan Publishing. (This book is in a series dealing with selected legal topics.)

*The English Legal System* (6th edition) by R J Walker (1985). Published by Butterworths.

*Firms With a Strong Interest in Legal Aid Work*, published by AGCAS, available from Careers Advisory Service, University of Sheffield, and many universities, polytechnics and colleges.

*A First Book of English Law* (7th edition) by O Hood Phillips and A H Hudson (revised 1988). Published by Sweet and Maxwell.

*A Law Degree – Then What?*, produced by the Scottish Young Lawyers' Association, 26 Drumsheugh Gardens, Edinburgh EH3 4YR.

*Learning the Law* (new edition) by Glanville Williams (1982). Published by Stevens.

*The Legal Profession*, produced by the Association of Graduate Careers Advisory Services, available from CSU Information Booklets, Crawford House, Precinct Centre, Manchester M13 9EP.

*The Legal System of Northern Ireland* by Brice Dickson (1984). Published by SLS Legal Publications (NI), Faculty of Law, The Queen's University of Belfast.

*Notes on Completing the Academic and Vocational Stages of Training*, produced by the Council of Legal Education, Inns of Court School of

Law, 4 Gray's Inn Place, London WCIR 5DX. Free of charge.

*Register of Graduate Employment and Training (ROGET)*, a booklet available from Careers Services at universities etc. Free of charge.

*The Scottish Legal System* by David M Walter (1981). Published by W Green & Son Ltd, Law Publishers, Edinburgh.

*The Scottish Universities Entrance Guide*, published by the Scottish Universities' Council or Entrance, Kinnersburn, Kennedy Gardens, St Andrews, Fife KY16 9DR.

*The Technique of Advocacy* by John Munkman (new edition) (1991). Published by Sweet and Maxwell.

*Women in the Legal Services* (1978). Published by the Equal Opportunities Commission, Overseas House, Quay Street, Manchester M3 3HN, and available free of charge from the Commission.

# Chapter 14

# Useful Addresses

The Association of Law Costs Draftsmen, The Secretary, 66 Ravensbourne Park Crescent, London SE6 4YP

The Association of Legal Secretaries, The Mill, Clymping Street, Clymping, Near Littlehampton, Sussex BN17 5RN; 0903 714276

The Association of Professional Shorthand Writers, c/o G Leigh, 6 Jelleyman Close, Blakebrook, Kidderminster DY11 6AI

The Bar Association for Commerce, Finance and Industry, 2 Plowden Buildings, Middle Temple Lane, London EC4Y 9AT; 071–353 4355

The Honorary Secretary, the Bar Association for Local Government and the Public Service, South Staffordshire District Council, Council Offices, Wolverhampton Road, Codsall, Wolverhampton WV8 1PX

The Bar Council, 11 South Square, Gray's Inn, London WC1R 5EL; 071–242 0082

Chambers and Partners, 74 Long Lane, London EC1A 9ET; 071–606 9371

The Chartered Institute of Patent Agents, Staple Inn Buildings South, High Holborn, London WC1V 7PZ; 071–405 9450

Citizens Advice Scotland, 26 George Square, Edinburgh EH8 9LD; 031–667 0156

The Civil Service Commission, Alencon Link, Basingstoke, Hampshire RG21 1JB; 0256 29222

The Civil Service Commission, Rosepark House, Upper Newtownards Road, Belfast BT4 3NR; 0231 84585

The Principal Chief Clerk and Clerk to the Committee of Magistrates for Inner London, Third Floor, North West Wing, Bush House, Aldwych, London WC2B 4PL

The Council for Licensed Conveyancers, Suite 3, Cairngorm House, 203 Marsh Wall, Docklands, London E14 9YT; 071–537 2953

The Council of Legal Education, 4 Gray's Inn Place, London WC1R 5DX; 071–404 5787

Establishment Officer, Crown Office, Regent Road, Edinburgh EH7 0LA; 031–557 3800

Establishment Officer, Department of the Director of Public Prosecutions, 4 Queen Anne's Gate, London SW1H 9AZ

The Faculty of Advocates, Advocates Library, Parliament House, 11 Parliament Square, Edinburgh EH1 1RF; 031–226 5071

Faculty Services Limited, Advocates Library, Parliament House, 11 Parliament Square, Edinburgh EH1 1RF; 031–226 5071

Greater London Citizens Advice Bureaux Service Limited, 136–144 City Road, London EC1V 2QN

The Home Office, C2 Division, 50 Queen Anne's Gate, London SW1H 9AT; 071–213 3000

The Honourable Society of the Inn of Court of Northern Ireland, The Royal Courts of Justice, Chichester Street, Belfast BT1 3JF; 0232 241523

Ilex Tutorial Services, Kempston Manor, Kempston, Bedford MK42 7AB

*The Inns:*

The Under Treasurer, The Honourable Society of Gray's Inn, Gray's Inn, London WC1R 5EU; 071–405 8164

The Sub Treasurer, The Honourable Society of Inner Temple, Inner Temple, London EC4Y 7HL; 071–353 8462

The Under Treasurer, The Honourable Society of Lincoln's Inn, Treasury Office, Lincoln's Inn, London WC2A 3TL; 071–405 0138

The Under Treasurer, The Honourable Society of Middle Temple, Middle Temple, London EC4Y 9AT; 071–353 4355

The Institute of Barristers' Clerks, 2 Garden Court, Ground Floor, Temple, London EC4Y 9BL; 071–583 5141

The Institute of Chartered Secretaries and Administrators, 16 Park Crescent, London W1N 4AH; 071–580 4741

The Institute of Legal Executives, Kempston Manor, Kempston, Bedford MK42 7AB; 0234 857711

The Institute of Shorthand Writers (write to The Careers Officer), 2 New Square, Lincoln's Inn, London WC2A 3RU; 071–405 9884

Law Centres' Federation, Duchess House, 18–19 Warren Street, London W1P 5DB; 071–387 8570

The Law Society, The Law Society's Hall, 113 Chancery Lane, London WC2A 1PL; 071–242 1222

The Law Society of Scotland, Rutland Exchange Box ED1, 26 Drumsheugh Gardens, Edinburgh EH3 7YR; 031–226 7411

The Law Society of Northern Ireland, Law Society House, 90–106 Victoria Street, Belfast BT1 3JZ; 0232 231614

(You may also wish to check with your local Law Society. Its address can be found in your local telephone directory.)

The Lord Chancellor's Department, Trevelyan House, 30 Great Peter Street, London SW1T 2BY; 071–210 3000

National Association of Citizens Advice Bureaux, 115–123 Pentonville Road, London N1 9LZ; 071–833 2181

Northern Ireland Association of Citizens Advice Bureaux, Regional Office, Newforge Lane, Belfast BT9 5NW; 0232 681117

Northern Ireland Court Service, Windsor House, 9–15 Bedford Street, Belfast BT2 7LT; 0232 328594

Scottish Education Department (Awards Branch), Haymarket House, Clifton Terrace, Edinburgh EH12 5DT

The Society of County Secretaries, The Secretary, Staffordshire County Council, County Building, Martin Street, Stafford ST16 2LH; 0785 223121

The Society of Public Notaries of London, Baltic Exchange Building, 24 St Mary Axe, London EC3A 8HD; 071–623 9477

The Universities' Central Council on Admissions, Rodney House, PO Box 28, Cheltenham, Gloucestershire GL50 1HY; 0242 222444

# Glossary

*action* Civil proceedings usually started by the issue of a writ, summons or petition

*advocate* A member of the legal profession in Scotland who has been admitted to Faculty of Advocates and whose principal function is to represent clients in court, on instructions from solicitors. This word is also used to denote any advocate, barrister or solicitor who represents and speaks of another in a court or other tribunal in any of the jurisdictions

*advocate's clerk* An administrator employed by Faculty Services Limited to organise the professional lives of advocates in Scotland

*appeal courts* These reconsider decisions of courts of first instance and consist of the Crown Courts, Divisional Court, Court of Appeal and House of Lords in England and Wales. The appeal courts in Scotland are the Inner House of the Court of Session, the High Court of Justiciary and in civil cases also the House of Lords in London. In Northern Ireland the appeal courts are the Assize Courts, the Divisional Court, the county courts and also the Court of Appeal and the House of Lords in London

*apprenticeship* Period of practical work and training under supervision in a solicitor's office (Scotland and Northern Ireland). See also *articles* and *indentures*

*articles* Period of practical work and training under supervision in a solicitor's office (England and Wales). See also *apprenticeship* and *indentures assize courts* Criminal appeal court in Northern Ireland something akin to the Crown Courts in England and Wales

*the Bar* Collective name for practising barristers

*The Bar Council* Autonomous body which represents and protects the interests of the Bar

*barrister* A member of the legal profession, in England and Wales and Northern Ireland, who has been called to the Bar and whose principal function is to work as an advocate on instructions received from solicitors

*barristers' clerk* An administrator who organises the professional lives of barristers in their chambers

*brief* Instructions from solicitors to barristers to appear in court to represent clients

*call* Law students are eligible for call to the Bar once they have passed the Bar Examination, provided they are at least 21 years old and have kept the required number of dining terms. Once called, a student becomes a barrister

*case law* Judicial decisions, a record of which is maintained in official law reports which can be referred to when later cases are heard

*Certificate of Professional Legal Studies* The professional qualification taken by both solicitors and barristers in Northern Ireland

*chambers* Barristers' private offices (England and Wales)

*chancery work* Cases involving wills, trusts and land, usually referred to the Chancery Division of the High Court

*civil proceedings* Cases brought by individuals or organisations against others, who have broken contractual obligations or committed torts

*commercial law* The body of law relating to business contracts, companies, partnerships, banking and trade

*Common Professional Exam (CPE)* The preliminary examination taken by non-law graduates and mature students training to be solicitors or barristers

*company secretary* The chief administrator of a limited company

*contentious matters* Cases which involve disputes between parties, usually resulting in litigation

*contract* A legally enforceable agreement made between two or more people

*conveyancing* The practice of transferring ownership of, and other rights in, property

*coroner* A barrister, solicitor or legally qualified doctor of five years' standing appointed to lead inquiries into sudden deaths etc (England and Wales and Northern Ireland)

*Council of Legal Education* The organisation which dictates the policy for the training of barristers (England and Wales)

*counsel* A barrister or barristers, or advocate or advocates. Usually refers to barristers or advocates in private practice

*county courts* Courts of first instance in England and Wales with limited civil jurisdiction

*court reporter* A person who attends court hearings to make a formal record of the proceedings, either in shorthand or by mechanical methods

*courts of first instance* These are the courts to which cases are first referred and consist, in England and Wales, of the High Court, Crown Courts, county courts and magistrates' courts. In Scotland the courts of first instance are Sheriff Courts, district courts and the Outer House of the

Court of Session. In Northern Ireland the courts of first instance are magistrates' courts, county courts and the High Court

*criminal proceedings* Cases brought on behalf of the Crown or by private individuals against people accused of committing offences which would render a convicted wrongdoer liable to punishment usually by fine or imprisonment

*Crown Courts* Courts with unlimited criminal jurisdiction (England and Wales)

*defendant* A person against whom a civil claim is brought, or a person who has been accused of a criminal offence

*delict* A breach of civil duty imposed by law (Scotland). See also *tort*

*devilling* A name given to pupillage in Scotland

*dining* Tradition of members of an Inn dining together. Otherwise known as 'keeping terms'

*Diploma in Legal Practice* The professional examination taken by both solicitors and advocates in Scotland

*district courts* Criminal courts of first instance in Scotland, something akin to the magistrates' court in England and Wales and Northern Ireland

*executor* A person appointed to carry out the instruction contained in a will

*Final Examination* The professional qualifying examination for solicitors qualifying in England and Wales, sometimes referred to as Solictors' Finals, which will be replaced by a new Legal Practice Course in 1993

*High Court* The court with unlimited civil jurisdiction (England, Wales and Northern Ireland)

*indentures* Another word used in Northern Ireland for apprenticeship

*Inns of Court* Four organisations with exclusive right to call to the Bar in England and Wales

*Inns of Court School of Law* Runs courses leading to the Bar Examination, directed by the Council of Legal Education (England and Wales)

*judges* Public officers appointed principally from the ranks of senior barristers and advocates who adjudicate cases and give a decision

*junior counsel* The name given to all barristers and advocates who are not Queen's Counsel

*justices' clerks* Barristers or solicitors of five years' qualified experience who are appointed to assist lay magistrates (JPs) with points of law when they are considering the cases before them.

*law costs draftsmen* People who prepare solicitors' bills in accordance with the rules and regulations governing solicitors' charges

*The Law Society, The Law Society of Scotland, The Law Society of Northern Ireland* The governing bodies of solicitors within the three jurisdictions being the organisations with the exclusive right to admit persons to the Roll of Solicitors within these jurisdictions

*legal aid* A scheme whereby people below a certain income and capital limit are entitled to apply to have their legal expenses partly paid out of public funds

*legal executive* An Associate or Fellow of the Institute of Legal Executives

*litigation* The practice of carrying on legal proceedings and bringing cases to court

*Magistrate* A judge in a magistrates' court. In England and Wales lay magistrates are called Justices of the Peace (JPs) and legally qualified magistrates are called stipendiary magistrates. All magistrates in Northern Ireland are legally qualified and are called Resident Magistrates (RMs)

*Masters* Name given in Northern Ireland to solicitors who supervise the work of apprentices. See *apprenticeship*

*Masters of the Bench* Senior members and governors of the Inns, often referred to as Benchers

*matrimonial law* The body of the law relating to divorce, separation, access to and custody of children

*muniments clerk* A person employed by a firm of solicitors to file deeds and documents held by the firm

*non-contentious matters* Cases which do not involve dispute between parties – such as conveyancing, probate and commercial drafting

*notary* A person authorised to draw up, witness and certify legal deeds and documents

*outdoor clerk* A person employed by a solicitor to issue court proceedings, lodge documents in court and obtain court appointments

*Outer House of the Court of Session* Civil Court of first instance in Scotland, something akin to the High Court in England and Wales

*partnership secretary* A person employed by a firm of solicitors as an administrator

*partnerships* Associations of two or more individuals who join together for the purposes of carrying on a business

*patent agent* A person qualified to register inventions on behalf of clients

*plaintiff* A person who brings a civil claim against another person

*Post-diploma training contract* The contract which an apprentice enters into with a principal (Scotland)

*principal* Name given in England and Wales and Scotland to solicitors who supervise the work of apprentices and articled clerks. See *apprenticeship* and *articles*

*probate* The practice of officially proving wills

*procedure* The formal steps involved in criminal or civil cases

*Procurator fiscal* Lawyer employed by the government in Scotland to investigate and prosecute crimes in the sheriff and district courts

*Professional Examination* Preliminary examination taken by non-law graduates and mature students in Scotland who wish to qualify as solicitors

*pupil* A barrister or advocate completing the year of pupillage

*pupillage* A year's compulsory working under supervision. The last part of the training of barristers or advocates who wish to work in private practice

*pupil master* A junior counsel who has completed five years' continuous practice, and who agrees to supervise the pupillage of a pupil

*Queen's Counsel (QC or Silk or Leading Counsel)* Senior barristers and advocates appointed in England and Wales by the Lord Chancellor, in Scotland by the Lord Justice General and in Northern Ireland by the Lord Chief Justice

*Sheriff Courts* Criminal and civil courts of first instance in Scotland. In dealing with criminal matters they are something akin to the Crown Courts of England and Wales and the assize courts of Northern Ireland.

*solicitor* A member of the legal profession who has been admitted to the Roll of Solicitors, in any of the three jurisdictions and whose principal functions are to advise clients and prepare paperwork for cases that will go to court

*solicitors' clerk* A person who helps a solicitor with legal work, but who is not a solicitor. Sometimes known as managing clerk, manager or clerk

*Solicitor's First Examination (SFE)* The first examination taken by school-leavers training to be solicitors (England and Wales)

*statute* An Act of Parliament

*summons* A document issued by a court requiring the person to whom it is addressed to attend before a judge or other court officer

*taxation (of costs)* The system whereby solicitors' fees are examined by the courts

*tenants* Barristers who have completed pupillage and who gain a permanent place in chambers (England and Wales)

*tort* A breach of civil duty imposed by law which gives the injured party a right to financial compensation (damages) (England and Wales). See also *delict*

*treasure trove* Money, gold, silver and jewels found hidden, whose ownership is unknown. Unless claimed by the owner, treasure trove belongs to the Crown

*will* The written instructions given by a person for the administration and distribution of his or her property on his or her death

*writ* A document issued by the High Court at the request of a plaintiff giving the defendant notice of the claim against him or her. A writ is the first step in a civil action begun in the High Court